Edward E. Hale

Our Christmas in a Palace

A Traveller's Story

Edward E. Hale

Our Christmas in a Palace
A Traveller's Story

ISBN/EAN: 9783337248130

Printed in Europe, USA, Canada, Australia, Japan

Cover: Foto ©Andreas Hilbeck / pixelio.de

More available books at **www.hansebooks.com**

Our Christmas in a Palace

A TRAVELLER'S STORY

BY

EDWARD EVERETT HALE

NEW YORK
FUNK & WAGNALLS, Publishers
10 AND 12 Dey Street
1883

Entered, according to Act of Congress, in the year 1883,
By FUNK & WAGNALLS,
In the Office of the Librarian of Congress at Washington, D. C.

THE admirable story of "Christmas in Cooney Camp," included in this volume, is kindly given me by my friend, Mr. Collingwood, who describes in it what he has seen and heard. It has never been published before. The other stories and sketches are my own.

EDWARD E. HALE.

ROXBURY, MASS., Oct. 1, 1883.

CONTENTS.

CHAPTER I.
Theodora Bourn and Jane Marhill.................... 7

CHAPTER II.
Paul Decker and Theodora Bourn. 23

CHAPTER III.
Snow-bound—Nahum Barrow's Revenge............... 48

CHAPTER IV.
Paul Decker's Story—Hands Off—Lulu's Doll................. 72

CHAPTER V.
Christmas Eve... 103

CHAPTER VI.
The Committee's Report and what followed.................... 106

CHAPTER VII.
Christmas Morning—Christmas in Cooney Camp—Christmas at Valley Forge... 109

CHAPTER VIII.
Hepzibah's Turkeys—Ideals—Nothing to Give................. 175

CHAPTER IX.

General Washington's Pig 246

CHAPTER THE LAST.

Paul Decker's Reflections—Breakfast 264

OUR CHRISTMAS IN A PALACE.

CHAPTER I.

THEODORA BOURN AND JANE MARHILL.

"COME out and walk, Mary; we shall have full twenty minutes. The conductor says fifteen, and you may be sure we shall not start till two."

Mary was glad enough to join him. As she crowded by the stove and porter's seat, at the end of the car, she proposed that he should ask little Black Ribbons to join them, and he did so. He went back to the place where Black Ribbons was sitting alone, touched his hat, and said:

"My wife is going to take a walk on the platform. Will you not join us?"

They had exchanged civilities with Black Ribbons before. But she was shy. They were happy in the joy of their wedding journey. Her seat was "three," quite at one end of the Pullman, and theirs was "twenty-one to twenty-four," quite at the other. Mary had offered her cold coffee at lunch and she had declined. The walk, therefore, was the first successful effort at anything like intimacy.

"Look there," said Hector, and he kicked with his foot an ingot of silver, which lay as heavy and motionless under the blow as if it had been spiked to the plank on which they stood. "If we were dishonest, we could hardly get that off—all three of us. And now the expressmen leave these three blocks, trusting not in our honesty, not in law or sheriff, not in any All-Seeing Eye, but simply in the dead weight of silver. That is the way of the world."

"The way of what world?"

"The way of this world. What I mean is that heavy people and things—people with much specific gravity—are let alone and prosper, as if dead weight were a merit, while light and airy people like us three, and elegant things like that silver when it shall have been drawn into threads, and moulded into butterflies for breast-pins, have to be watched and tended and daintily lifted from place to place. Now, there is our Cæsar Ganymede, the Pullman porter, sadly looking upon you now, he is so afraid you will be left, Mary."

"You would like to go as freight?" said Mary.

"Not quite that. For then they would lay me on my back, and put two tea-chests on me, and a log of red-wood on them, and these ingots of silver on them, and lock the car door for ten days."

"You would arrive breathless, like a messenger in a novel."

"Yes, and my clothes would need brushing. But we might all three have been sent not as freight, but as parcels, by Adams's Express. We could have been tied up in brown paper, like dolls. They could have marked us, 'This side up with care.' We should go by 'great speed,' as they say in France. We should not have to pay a cabman when we arrived in Columbus, and we should have, to spend at the theatre, all the money these blessed through tickets have cost us."

"Minus what we paid the expressman."

"No, madam. For that we have provided independently. For the hard-earned specie which I gave to yonder bloated conductor for our Pullman section, and which our friend here has paid for hers, would more than satisfy the greed of the express company. I am tall but thin. I should not measure more than six cubic feet. I should first tie up both you ladies back to back, and you would not together measure more than eight feet. It is not too late now. I will go and speak to the express agent."

And he pretended to leave them. But at this moment the train conductor touched his hat, and said : "Please get on board again, sir. I shall start the train a little before time. It is beginning to snow above us, and my plough is at station one hundred and three. I should rather be there before the snow gathers."

So they tumbled into the car. But in this nonsense of Hector's the ice was broken, and Mary and Black Ribbons took seats twenty-three and twenty-four, when they returned to the car, while Hector went forward and found company in the smoking-car.

Black Ribbons proved to be going to the East for the first time she could remember. Her father had been a superintendent in a queer sort of mine, if you may so call it, which was covered by every tide of the Pacific, twice in twenty-four hours. When the waters receded, they could work the gold-besprent sand. When the waters gathered again, they slept, or ate, or played poker, I suppose. Mining with such limitations had not rendered much profit. The child who grew up in such queer surroundings was by far the best dividend her father and mother had won from them.

At last he had died, a disappointed man. Her mother could not "boss" a gang of workmen, and had, unwillingly enough, left their not uncomfortable home by the sea for the closer life of Sacramento, where she had tried the doubtful career of a boarding-house keeper. In a fitful way the two had kept the wolf from the door for a year or more; but that fight ended with the sudden death of the widow. She had left her daughter for a day and night only. The first news the poor girl had was that her mother was dead. The next was when the cold body was brought home. Crossing the ferry from San Francisco to Oakland, the steamer had come to grief.

"A slight accident," said the evening paper. "Travel was suspended only till the boat could be hauled into dock and her place taken by the Golden City. No person was injured, with the exception of one of the passengers, a lady, name unknown. She was taken to the city hospital."

She died before she arrived there, and Theodora, the next day, stood at the door of her home to receive her mother's dead body.

"Yes; everybody was kind. They were very kind. I should have died, you know, if they had not been kind. I had twenty homes open to me. But I could not stay in them always, you know. They have all helped me, all through. There are the very nicest people in all the world in Sacramento. But, of course, I could not keep the boarders. Mr. Flynn arranged about the lease, and then they had an auction and sold all our things; that was the very worst—and—well—there have been endless letters—then it was settled that I should go to my mother's brother's home for this winter. His farm is in Piqua, or at least it is between Piqua and Troy. Do you know any one in Piqua? I heard you speak of Columbus."

No; Mary knew nobody in Piqua. Five seconds before she had not known that there was any such place as Piqua in the world. But with the wisdom and confidence of the married state, as one who knew the world and what was in it, she ventured to assure Mary that she doubted not there were very nice people and very good social order in Piqua. Her husband was an Ohio man, or had friends in Ohio, and doubtless he was acquainted in Piqua.

Had Theodora more experience in life, she would have known, from the intonation with which Mary uttered the word "husband," that she was not much accustomed to its use. Indeed, there was a certain importance in the tone, as if she had said " His Serene Eminence," or "His Royal Majesty," as if this husband was distinct from all the other husbands, and as if Theodora of course knew the distinction. The truth was that he was a husband of four days and one hour's standing, and Mary had had no occasion to call him by his official title till this moment.

As for his having "friends in Ohio," it was true that Douglas, one of his college friends, lived in Columbus, and had asked the bride and bridegroom to visit him on their way to their home in Penn Yan. But Mary wanted to put as bright a face on things as she could do.

In such confidences, the two girls hardly noticed how the snow closed in around them. Little they heeded it, indeed, that the train arrived at one hundred and three an hour and twenty minutes after time.

Hector bustled in then, and said: "Now we are all right; we have our snow-plough, and they say there is less snow after we cross the next divide."

"All right! has anything been wrong?"

"Oh, no—not wrong, you know; only we are a little late here. Snow clogged under the drivers. Road very rough. But it is all over now. We shall make up the time before we come to the Junction.

And then he gave Mary a chance to ask him whom he knew at Troy or at Piqua.

Theodora Bourn, the young girl whom they had called Black Ribbons, felt that the world was a new world after the bride and bridegroom had admitted her into their little travelling party. She had left Sacramento not quite alone. A Mr. Wilcox, who was going east, had been made to say that he would see to her. But even before they arrived at Ogden, Mr. Wilcox had broken down with a headache so heavy and a pulse so high, that a jury of passengers had pronounced unanimously that he must stop there, and Theodora had found that he was in her charge—not she in his. The poor man had been able to hunt up a business correspondent in Ogden, and with the large and cheerful hospitality of the West, the people summoned had made him comfortable enough. But after this ill-omened beginning, Black Ribbons, who would have known herself better as Theodora Bourn, was taken to the New York Express, and found herself in seat number three of the Pullman, with the prospect of three or four days without any companion. Hector Van Sandfoord and his pretty bride had come on board at Cheyenne City, where they had stayed over a day to break the strain of their voyage eastward. Now that Theodora could hear the sound of her own voice and of somebody's besides, her spirits rose, and she felt that all would go well.

The train was a singularly small one. Indeed, the season, as we found, was not propitious for long travelling. One car, for way travellers mostly, picked up a handful of passengers now and then, and dropped another handful. In the smoking-car there would congregate a group of card-players; and this was, on the whole, the most densely peopled car on the train. A dining-room and kitchen followed the Pullman palace, as that followed the more plebeian carriages. If the snow would only hold off, there would be no difficulty in making the time.

Our three friends went back to supper together, about half-past six, having talked in the darkness as long as the waiters would let them, that the evening might seem the shorter. As they sat down at the pretty table, Theodora said:

"My great grief in this delay at Ogden is that it keeps me on the road all Christmas day. I hoped even against hope, and had taken it for granted that I could spend the end of my Christmas at Piqua. It will seem forlorn enough to spend the whole day in the train. But there is no help for that now."

"Help, my dear child! You will not travel an inch on Christmas. You will stop with us at Council Bluffs, and go down with us to the Corneaus at Hastings. I do not know what the connection is. Hector is not sure. But it is only twenty miles. We shall be there in time to hang up our stockings."

"Who are the Corneaus? Why, it seems as if we had known you so long that you must know. The Corneaus are— Well, Hector, tell her who the Corneaus are."

"Whoever they are," replied poor Theodora with a little reserve, "they are not expecting to have you bring every waif you pick up on the railroad to their Christmas party."

"Not expecting it? Queer people, if they did not expect it! My dear Theodora, where have you lived all your life? If you had tried life at a Mission from the time you were one—till—till—"

"Till you became a married lady of dignity and knowledge of the world," said Hector, interrupting her, "if you were this, Miss Bourn, you would know that the Corneaus, who live two or three miles out from Hastings, would never speak to me again, if my wife once let slip that we had let Miss Theodora Bourn go on her way alone. Let me give you the thigh of this chicken. You don't wish gravy? You are the first woman who ever refused it. To think of the rage of the Corneaus, if you do not stop at their house at Christmas!"

And so little Theodora was fairly enfolded into the travelling bridal party, and was to take the chances of life with them.

They went back into the palace, and they tried a game of euchre with a dummy. But the game palled, and seemed to be rather in the way. Mrs. Fréchette and her husband, with whom they had passed some civilities before, came up and took the seats opposite twenty-three and twenty-four, and, as it happened—they hardly knew why—there came a very long post at a station, so that the car was wholly still. They could, therefore, now talk across the passage-way without difficulty, and all became very intimate.

"You say you thought you should not have money enough for your tickets," said Mrs. Fréchette, in comment on some story of Theodora Bourn.

"Do you not know how young ladies travel without money?"

"They make their husbands pay," said Mr. Fréchette.

"Not at all," said his wife. "It is much simpler. How do you suppose Scheherezade travelled—the woman in the Arabian Nights? Do you think she bought a through ticket?"

"Not much," said Mary. "I always heard that she sat on a carpet and it carried her. I wonder if this carpet would fly if we took it out of the car."

"Nonsense," said Mrs. Fréchette; "she told stories to the conductors. She was what they call a deadhead."

"I always understood that they called them tramps, when they came with a pack of lies."

"Tom, hold your tongue! I tell you that Scheherezade's plan has been transferred to our times and ways. It tells all about it here. If Cæsar there will only light up the side-light I will read it to you."

And the jolly Mrs. Fréchette, in triumph, dug from the bottom of her lunch-basket a badly worn, not to say somewhat greasy copy of the *Cottage Hearth*.

"I keep it," said she, "lest Tom be left over at a way-station, as he will be some day, and I need to work my passage."

So, as soon as Cæsar had lighted up, she read:

JANE MARHILL'S STORY.

Jane Marhill had graduated at the Hamilton Academy with all the honors. She and the other girls and the first class had sat up half the night talking with each other. Miss Norton, the mistress of the school, was always very good to the girls at parting, and she had a little private breakfast party in her own room the last morning. But this would not last forever, and at last good, kind Dr. Wistar came round in his own buggy to take Jane to the train. She kissed good-by to all. "Be sure you are in time with the trunk, Cicero!" And Cicero said, "Sartin, Miss Jane, the hoss is here," and by way of emphasis took Jane's hand-bag also. The girl was confused with so many good-bys, and gave it to him quite unconsciously.

Often and often had she a chance to regret this. For on that bit of gallantry of Cicero's hinged all her misfortunes. Dr. Wistar bade her good-by at the station. The train was absolutely on time. Cicero had relied on its being ten minutes late, as usual, and when "All on board" was sounded, Jane stood without her trunk and without her satchel.

But she had her ticket; what should she care if she came home with her luggage a day behind her? She charged Mr. Treby, the station-master, who was a tried friend of all the girls, to send both pieces after her on the first train.

"All right, Miss Jane. I will double-check them, and you will have them to-morrow morning."

So Jane blithely entered the car, little thinking at the moment what was before her.

When the conductor asked her for her ticket, Jane gave it to him for his "punch," and then recollected, for the first time, that it only took her to the junction at Whipple. At Whipple they would all have to wait for the Cattaraugus and Opelousas express. Jane knew that junction only too well. She had waited there four times a year for five years. They would arrive there at dark, and the express was due about half an hour after they came in. All this Jane knew and was prepared for. But the dreadful memory which shocked her, from her gulping throat to her beating heart, was that her purse was in the fatal hand-bag which she had trusted to Cicero, and that she had with her not one cent for her expenses after this very moment of her life !

Was there, perhaps, some one in the train from whom Jane might borrow ?

Not a man, not a woman ! If that horrid Schaus of the bee-hive shop had been on his way to New York, Jane would have abased herself. If only Miss Marion, the head of the rival Female College, had been there she would have done it. But there had been no passenger except herself at Gallatin, which was the seat of Hamilton Academy and the Female College, and all the other people seemed to be butchers on their way from Brighton. "Perhaps it is as well," said Jane. "Did not Dr. Withers charge us in his farewell sermon never to borrow? If only I could walk home from Whipple!" But one cannot walk one hundred and twenty miles in one evening.

On the seat in front of her was a little German girl who was ticketed, by a visible card pinned upon her frock, to Littleton, not twenty-five miles from Jane's home.

To divert herself from the sense of her misery, Jane asked the girl to sit with her, and remembered then, with another great choke, how warm and nice were the crullers in the lost bag, and how gladly she would have treated the child with them. Failing the crullers she asked the child if she could make paper dolls. It proved that the little waif could not speak English. Jenny profited by the occasion to air and exercise her

German conversation. Before long she had her scissors at work cutting out dolls, cats and dogs, roebucks and cows, trees and houses, from a handbill which advertised lunch on the ferry-boat. Alas, no lunch for Jane that day! But the child was grateful to her, and she was grateful to the child.

And so she rushed on at a rapid speed, nearer and nearer to her doom!

"Whipple Junction! Change for stations on Cattaraugus and Opelousas." Jane left her home, and so did Gretchen. Jane was and knew she was a vagabond. She had no money and no visible means of support. She was a tramp—Gretchen at her side was a bloated millionaire in the comparison.

The conductor had Gretchen's lot intrusted to him. He came to direct her where to buy her ticket—was relieved to find Jenny in charge, and said hastily, "The girl is to go to Littleton. She needs a new ticket here." Poor Jenny! She led the girl to the ticket window, waited in the queue, bought the ticket with the money Gretchen furnished, and gave back to Gretchen the precious change—six dollars and forty cents. Had ever money seemed so precious!

Would she confide in Gretchen? Would she borrow from her?

That would seem too *thin*, the girl would have said, had the language of Hamilton Academy furnished her with so convenient a term. Come what would she would not borrow. But she did turn to the ticket-seller.

"Is the express on time?"

"No, Miss; it was forty-seven minutes late at Sedgemoor. They will make up some of it, but not all."

As she turned from the ticket-office she saw the placard, brightly lighted, which read :

"NOTICE TO LOAFERS."

" All loafing in this room is prohibited by law." And then followed the section of the act aimed at all persons who, "without right," haunt railway stations.

But Jane rose superior to the insinuation. The smile of victory was on her face now. For, with the words of the ticket-seller, light had dawned on her.

She was no longer a loafer. She had found a vocation !

She did not, however, as yet, enter upon its exercise.

Skilfully she reserved herself, till she saw and knew that the other passengers waiting for the express were becoming desperate at their detention.

At that junction—as at most junctions—the lamps are so high and so bad that no one can read. The seats are so nailed to the floor, that you cannot make groups for conversation, or even for playing at cards. Grimly the waiting throng sat or stood. Now one walked on the platform in the drizzly rain. Now he came back to the misery of the half-lighted room. All watched the clock, which in the deadness of the place almost stopped, but crawled on enough to make it sure that the machinery was not accountable for the slowness of time.

Jane felt at last that her moment had come.

With the same courage which she had pretended the day before, on the stage at the exhibition, she stepped forward—holding the hand of little Gretchen—and said to the astonished detained people :

"Ladies and gentlemen, the time passes very slowly. It has been suggested that I should—TELL A STORY!"

The effective pause just before the proposal, wrought its perfect work, and the proposal was received with hearty applause. The applause encouraged Jenny, and she began.

The girl had had practice enough. Often and often had she told stories to the girls at the Academy, while they gladly copied out her exercises for her in return, from her rough notes.

She began with an English steamer sailing from the Mersey. She described, realistically, her own experiences of a year before, when she came home with her father and mother from a summer tour. But now, in her story, the travellers were a German workman, his wife and daughter, who had second-class passages. She portrayed the second cabin. She just entered into its intrigues and politics, but not far. Of a sudden— as all slept on board in the night—shouts overhead: the helm put down hard! Too late—the ship crashes against ice! The stewards rush through the cabins summoning all to rise. They dress in wild haste. They stagger on deck to be told off to the boats. The child is parted from her father and mother! She is fairly thrown into the surgeon's boat! The boat is cast off.

And here the story-teller paused.

To the baggage-master, who was listening in the throng: "Would you have the kindness to bring me a cup of water?"

Then, in German to Gretchen: "Take off your hat and pass it to the gentlemen and ladies." Then to the assembly: "Perhaps they will like to help a poor traveller on her way."

The child supposed this might be the custom of a new country, in which she had been a citizen now for twenty-six hours.

She did as she was bidden. A jolly old Texan, whom she touched first, modestly, dropped a silver dollar in the hat. One and another of the detained fumbled in the change pocket of his coat, one and another lady dived into her travelling-bag. Jane did not wait for the little girl to come back with her collections, but went on as if indifferent.

"Quartermaster, is your boat clear?"

"Aye, aye, sir!"

"And you, Mr. Flagg?"

"Aye, aye, sir!"—

But at this moment the distant scream of a whistle. The baggage-master appeared with his mug of water.

"The train is in sight, Miss. They have made up their time."

And, with the word, Jane's audience melted away. She was left alone with Gretchen.

With her well-earned travel-gelt she turned to the window, and asked boldly for her ticket.

The clerk, another man from the one she saw before, looked at the paper pinned upon the window-frame, and said:

"Is this Miss Marhill?"

"Why, yes," replied Jane.

"Miss Marhill, your father is on the train. He is coming up from Lawrence. He left word this morning that he has your ticket and you were to buy none."

So Jane took Gretchen into the palace car, as the train stopped, and in a moment was in her father's arms.

*　　*　　*　　*　　*　　*

Everybody laughed heartily at the end of Mrs. Fréchette's little story. But Tom, her husband, said:
"It ends like all the rest of them, I observe.
"The new invention is very fine.
"But I see that, all the same, the man pays for the tickets."

And on this they told Cæsar that he might make up the berths. The men went forward to see what was the cause of the detention. Theodora and Mary kissed each other, and in an hour every one on the train, except the working hands, was sleeping soundly—more soundly, indeed, than is usual on a train.

CHAPTER II.

PAUL DECKER AND THEODORA BOURN.

THE next morning Cæsar took a hint from the P. P. C., which letters mean Pullman Palace Conductor. This right worthy commander told Cæsar there was no need of waking the sleepers; and the sleepers, most of whom had slept at the rate of thirty-five miles an hour for the last two or three nights before, finding themselves in perfect stillness and well-nigh perfect darkness, availed themselves of the occasion, and made up for past deficiencies.

When, at eight o'clock, one and another began to find themselves wakeful, the mystery of silence and stillness was explained. The train was switched off the main track at the Brady Island station, and had been for hours. Something had happened at the eastward—no one knew what. The telegraph answered to no appeals except from the west. We could not even hear from Council Bluffs by the reverse way of Denver and the K. P. R., as we tried to do.

"We shall have to ride a little way on Christmas morning, after all, Miss Bourn, if your scruples will permit. We shall hardly leave the Bluffs this afternoon, as I had promised you."

And so Hector and Mary and Theodora went back to breakfast. They found George Hackmetack and the Fréchettes in the breakfast car already, and most of the other palace people soon reported. No morning newspaper, but no lack of topics for talk in the discussion of the probabilities of the delay.

As it proved, the delay gave us two pleasant additions to our party, and, indeed, our one adventure.

No one needed to hurry at breakfast, more than they had hurried in waking. One by one the gentlemen strayed out for their cigars, and all the ladies, as it happened, were left with Van Sandfoord alone, chatting over grapes and coffee. It was nearly ten o'clock when Cæsar came back to see what had happened to his gentlemen and ladies, and the little group then made their way slowly forward. Van Sandfoord left the ladies in the palace, and went out upon the little platform of the station.

He was walking with a ranchman, whom he met there, when Cæsar came up, a good deal excited:

"Your lady, sar, say the other lady lost—little black bonnet lady lost—not come back from breakfuss."

"Lost, Cæsar!" cried Hector, laughing. "How can she be lost in two cars? I wish there were more chance for all of us to be lost." But he hurried back to see what his wife's message really was, and found that Cæsar had not blundered.

The women had gathered by themselves — had brought out books and work. Mrs. Fréchette had started a little water-color sketch, and things began to seem sociable, when they had noticed that Theodora did not appear. Mary Van Sandfoord sent Cæsar back to the breakfast-room, to ask her to come and see how comfortable they were, and she was not there. Some one suggested that she had friends forward; but they were worried now, and Cæsar was sent forward in vain.

Hector was sure that she had not passed him or appeared on the station platform, and so were all the gentlemen who had been grouped and smoking there. Every search and even every guess was exhausted in dumb wonder, when from the other side of the snow-bound station we were loudly hailed. Every one ran round the corner, and we met a vigorous young man with poor Theodora unconscious in his arms. He was stepping slowly on snow-shoes, and followed by a companion.

"Have you so many women here that you leave them lying alone in the snow?" he said, as he carried his charge into the open door-way of the station.

Just where the heaviest drift formed, high and treacherous against the bare open way left by the gale, as it swept round the corner of the house, the poor girl had fallen and lay wholly senseless when he found her. It proved, when she came to herself, that as she crossed from the kitchen to the palace—how easy that transition seems sometimes!—her veil had blown from her hand, and lay in tantalizing neighborhood on the bare ground below. It was nothing for the girl to step down for it. But, as she stepped, it was nothing for the veil to fly a few yards from her. She followed as promptly—followed without a Yankee girl's knowledge of snow, wholly ignorant of the capacities of a snow-drift—made two fatal steps into a bed two or three feet deep, which yielded immediately under her, fell forward on her face, struggled vainly with both hands and arms, and in a few moments forgot everything.

It was, as we guessed, within five minutes or ten that she was telling us this, while Mrs. Fréchette chafed one arm, and Mary Van Sandfoord one foot, as she sat in the one arm-chair of the "Ladies' Room."

The knights who had come to the rescue so fortunately were Fergus Menet and one of his chemists, a young fellow named Decker.

·Luckily for Theodora, they had ridden across from some explorations they had been making, to strike our train, but had been hindered by the snow—had had to give up their horses and take to snow-shoes.

Luckily for them our train was half a day or less behind time.

As they came up they saw our lazy engine and our silent cars, with mingled joy and terror, for they could not see a living being to signal, yet at any moment the train might move from them.

Just as Decker, in advance, was hailing the station, he saw the corner of Theodora's frock straying out from the snow. The unconscious girl was already nearly covered by the rapid drift.

It needed then but a moment for these strong men to uncover her, and bring her into the station-house.

Theodora was taken up into the little state-room of the Pullman, so soon as her blood was well started. Mrs. Fréchette and Mary shut themselves in with her, and presided over the cares of her recovery. Cæsar was sent forward with her check for her trunk, which was brought and opened in the palace ; and, in the course of half an hour, she appeared again. She was very much mortified at making so much fuss ; very pretty, nicely and dryly dressed, and just as well as if she had had the good luck to take a good cold sponge bath before she dressed—a bit of luxury which had been denied to all the rest of us.

"And to think," cried Mary, "of being rescued and restored by the great Fergus Menet himself."

For Mary had found out from her husband who the new-comers were.

Theodora asked who "the great Fergus Menet" was?

"Do you not know who Fergus Menet is? A California girl not know Fergus Menet? Did you ever hear of Napoleon Bonaparte or of Queen Victoria?"

"I think I once heard a Chinaman speak of Queen Victoria. But who is the other one? Was he not the King of the Cannibal Islands?"

"Oh, Theodora, you are joking. Why, Fergus Menet, he is 'M., P. & V.'—'Menet, Perry, and Ville Fosse.' You hardly ever see a block of silver our way but is marked 'M., P. & V.' And he is as good as he is rich, and all women ought to know about him. When you are rested, I will tell you all his story—"

"Rested? Dear Mrs. Van Sandfoord, I am rested now. Was ever your Queen· Victoria—if that is her name—more comfortable in Windsor?"

Pretty girl, she might well say so. Cæsar had opened out 17, 18, 19, and 20. He had brought in, I know not how many pillows, and heaped them up, as loves in the pictures heap cushions on the barge for Cleopatra. And there our rosy, eager, modest Theodora half lay and half sat, with every conceivable colored rug which the stores of all the party could produce piled round her, while the rich crimson of the Pullman blankets gave the dominating color for the picture.

"There is no time like this," said Theodora, "if it would not tire you to tell us."

"Tire me! Such things do not tire me. Besides, it is all written down."

And Mrs. Van Sandfoord opened her extensor case. It was packed woman-fashion with all Mary's treasures. Her Thomas à Kempis, and her diamond brooch, and her little brother's picture, and her last letter from her mother, kissed one another amicably, and at the bottom of the whole, in a yellow envelope, just as Miss Norton had sent it to her from Gallatin, was the story of Fergus Menet and Ellen Markley. As the *Independent* people had named it, it was called

TOGETHER.

I. NEW PADUA.

"SHALL you go to your uncle's for your Thanksgiving dinner?"

Ellen asked this question a little timidly.

"No," said Fergus, rather shortly ; and then he added, with an artificial smile : "I shall take pot-luck here with Mrs. Odonto, unless your aunt asks me."

Mrs. Odonto kept the boarding-house at which Fergus and Ellen both lived.

"No," said Ellen—and her smile was half a smile only, and her eyes looked a little wet—"my aunt will not ask you ; for—for—I have told her that I should not accept her invitation."

Fergus fairly laughed this time.

"Have you had a row there? I have had a row with my uncle."

Fergus and Ellen were engaged to be married, and had been for a year past. He was the assistant teacher in chemistry in the State Agricultural College.

This meant that he opened and shut the shutters, according as the professor's experiments required sun or shade, and that he cleared up the broken glass and other fragments when the professor was done. The place was rather a galling one for Fergus, who knew perhaps as much of the new chemistry as the professor did. As for Ellen, she was an assistant teacher in the same college ; for the State Agricultural College was also the State University, and in that State co-education existed. So Ellen taught young men and young women to square the hypothenuse and to work out the binomial theorem; while in the basement Fergus Menet swept up the fragments, and chafed when the professor failed in his experiments.

The drawback about the Thanksgiving dinner began deeper down than you might guess. Fergus had made an evening call at his uncle's, knowing that he would be welcome on Thanksgiving day, and hoping, nay expecting, that they would ask Ellen Markley to come with him. His engagement to her was perfectly understood. His aunt had called on Ellen, and Ellen had returned the call. Instead of this his aunt had made an excuse to be alone with him. Then she had said, half in joke and half in earnest, as it seemed, that Miss Gholson, from Albany, was coming to visit her ; that Miss Gholson had been very much interested in Fergus when he spoke at Saratoga, at the Association ; that she had spoken of him several times, as if she remembered him ; that she had an immense fortune in her own right ; and that if Fergus would "follow his hand," as his aunt elegantly said, he could win Miss Gholson's and could be independent for life. In reply to all this, Fergus had said, very simply at first, that he was engaged to the sweetest girl in the world ; and when his aunt intimated that such things meant nothing with young people, Fergus had flared up and gone away in a rage. This rage had not subsided when Ellen Markley asked him, as you know, if he should go to his uncle's for his Thanksgiving dinner.

All this, of course, Ellen did not understand. Fergus would not insult her by telling her. But what Ellen did understand, and had understood for weeks, was that she would not taste salt nor turkey on Thanksgiving day at the stately mansion of the Robervals. The Robervals were old Huguenot people. They lived four miles out from New Padua, in an elegant way. Mrs. Roberval was Ellen's aunt; and last year Ellen was there at Thanksgiving and at Christmas. But it happened, oddly enough, that Mrs. Roberval had been making a match for Ellen just about the time her engagement for Fergus came on. The stately and rich Mr. Arbuthnot, the great Connecticut manufacturer, had seen Ellen at the Robervals', had admired her, had offered himself, and had been refused. But Mrs Roberval had told him that faint heart never won fair lady, and he could not give up. And an eager letter had come from him, and Mrs. Roberval had shown it to Ellen and had made her cry. And Ellen had said to herself that she would not go to Rochelle House to dine for all the world, if they did not ask Fergus; and, as Ellen knew, they were as likely to ask Sitting Bull.

So was it that, for reasons not dissimilar, these two young people were to have their Thanksgiving dinner with such company as Mrs. Odonto might supply, at the boarding-house table.

II. A THANKSGIVING DINNER.

I do not know. What I do not know is this: whether Mrs. Odonto was glad or sorry that Fergus Menet and Ellen Markley notified her that they should dine at the boarding-house.

What I do know is: that Rose Finegan, the cook, expected a holiday that day, and that Mary Maginnis, the table-girl, was going to the Mills for the day; so

I think that Mrs. Odonto hoped that all the boarders would dine away from what she was pleased to call "home." I am sure none of the boarders called it so.

However, Mrs. Odonto bore up bravely, and made no sign of anxiety or regret, though she knew that the Thanksgiving dinner would have to be cooked by her own red right-hand.

But when Ellen heard that Mrs. Odonto's brigadier and major-generals were to desert her, or to assume other fields of duty, she changed her plans, and she persuaded Fergus to change his. She did not think it at all "nice" that Mrs. Odonto should have to slave and slave just to get them a dinner ; so she proposed that they should turn Mrs. Odonto out of doors also. She would ask Minna Ville-Fosse, who was the German teacher in the Agricultural College, to come and dine with them ; and she and Minna would cook the dinner. If Fergus were to marry her, she said, it was but right that he should know whether she could cook a dinner. As for him, he might ask home any gentleman he liked. He should be a nice gentleman, Ellen said, who would like to talk with Minna, who was a very charming girl.

Fergus grumbled a little at the necessity of being hospitable. But Ellen told him—what he knew very well before—that there was no Thanksgiving unless they shared what was provided ; and intimated that, if she and he spent the day together, with or without Mrs. Odonto's company, they might become tired of each other too soon. It ended, of course, in her having her own way. Mrs. Odonto said she would take the morning car for New Herkimer, and the young people were to work their own sweet will in the kitchen and dining-room. Nay, before Thanksgiving day came, the kitchen was given over on Tuesday afternoon to Ellen and to her friend Minna. And there, in the secrecy of a cabbala whose oracles no man shall interpret, they created pies and tarts and jellies, now of Yankee, now of German workmanship—enough, one would have said, for a dinner of twenty covers; but in truth all prepared for one of four.

Fergus hesitated a little about the guest he should bring, to be agreeable to the Fraulein Minna. College professors, resident graduates, unmarried ministers in the town passed in procession before his mind, as he determined which of them should have the honor of being selected as fourth hand in this select game of Thanksgiving day. But Fergus also was under the influence of the day; and he finally gave his invitation, not to one of these people who were to choose between four or five parties, but to a new-found friend of his, whose room was in the attic of the Too-Good House, and who would have taken his chance at the stage dinner of that inn, had not Fergus remembered him. This was a seedy-looking man, named Perry, whom Fergus had found at the Union. At the Union he had a sort of natural history class, made up of factory hands and shop clerks, whom he was initiating into the mysteries of mineralogy and geology. Fergus had been drawn toward him since the first time he saw him. Perry had asked him to let him use the laboratory, to make some rather intricate examinations of some bog-ore the boys had brought back from a vacation ramble. The man seemed to have had a specialist's training. Very crude in some things he was, very shrewd in others. He was very lonely in the town, and, as Fergus knew, would hardly call any one his friend excepting him. But Perry knew very well what Thanksgiving day was. Even in his loneliness he had found it the loneliest day in the year, ever since he had been in America ; and the tears fairly stood in his eyes when he received and accepted Fergus's invitation.

Fergus compelled Perry to go to "meeting" with him. No man would dare say whether Perry had fulfilled righteousness in that way before since he had lived in New Padua. But they heard Mr. Cross preach a sermon on the Indian policy of the General Government, they put their surplus earnings into the contribution-box, and then, as instructed by the women folk, they took a long walk before they returned to dinner. They found the table set ; and in a little while the ladies came in, with their faces aglow, but not too much aglow, and condescended to let the gentlemen bring in the heavy turkey and the chicken-pie, while they followed with trays laden with side-dishes. In this self-service there was quite frolic enough to break the ice. Fergus asked a blessing with good heart, and from Boothia Felix to the Farallones Islands there was not a jollier Thanksgiving dinner that day than this proved to be.

Minna Ville-Fosse was, indeed, what Ellen had represented her — a sweet, pretty girl. French blood mixed with German in her blushes, and French brightness and German sense in her talk. Her English was, like Kossuth's, just broken enough and unidiomatic enough to be suggestive and entertaining. As for Perry, you never knew where to find him. The New Education, which is just now showing its results, certainly brings curiosity and surprise into conversation. You never know what a man will understand nor where his mind will be a blank. Mr. Perry sat perfectly silent when the others tried some quite familiar themes of literature. On the other hand, he would come out with a world of curious and entertaining information about things where archangels might be pardoned for ignorance.

Of all which talk, now very serious and now very merry, the only part which much concerns this story fell after dinner, when they were wasting Mrs. Odonto's hard cut logs in a great open fireplace in her parlor. Fergus had been grinding an axe by making Minna Ville-Fosse explain to him some phrases in his German mining-books. She proved to be an expert of the hundred-thousandth power.

"How in the world did you know all these crack-jaw words?" cried he, at last.

"Why not? How should I know any other words? I have lived at Freiberg till I was fifteen. My father was a superintendent of mines. My grandfather was a famous mining engineer. All my dear brothers are underground at this moment, I suppose."

Mr. Perry left talking with Ellen, almost rudely, and directed his attention to the book and the talk. In a minute the reason appeared. He was a Welshman. All his earlier life had been spent in Swansea. The name of Ville-Fosse was as familiar to him as the name of Worth is to a Baltimore belle or of Edwards to an Andover student; and, without thinking much of his manners, he turned to listen.

Then what talk there was about schists, and gangues, and carbonates, and pyrites; about Himmelsfürst, and Veta Grande, and Veta Madre; about limestone and fluxes, and rubbish, what had been done and what might be done and what ought to be done, till Ellen declared herself disgusted. She would not be left out in the cold, she said. She opened Mrs. Odonto's card table, and made them, willy-nilly, give up their beloved assays and reductions. She produced a new pack of cards, and taught them all to play ombre, which was the game of the Rape of the Lock. Ombre is whist as whist would be under a despot. Whist is ombre where the despot has had his head cut off, and peasants, merchants, priests, and soldiers, or clubs, diamonds, hearts, and spades, are equal in their rights before the law. But Ellen made them play ombre. Most women, in their heart of hearts, incline for despotism in government.

III. PROSPECTING.

And this is all that can be told of that gay little picnic dinner-party. What grew out of it all seemed simple enough at the time. When Fergus found that Mr. Perry had spent all his early life in the various grades of smelting works in Swansea, he told him that New Padua was no place for him, which, alas! poor Perry knew well enough already. Fergus told Perry that he ought to be in Arizona. He showed him, in the college library, in Allegre and Venegas, the evidence that there was a time when the chief fountain of Spanish wealth flowed in silver from far-off Arizona. The attic of the Too-Good House was no place for him, while sulphurets and carbonates were waiting for him to torture them under a sky so delicious. In Sonora, just over the border, was found the largest nugget of silver ever seen, preserved perhaps to this hour in some museum in Spain. That did not weigh quite three thousand pounds, and probably was not worth fifty thousand dollars. "But you shall find a bigger one," said Fergus. "You shall send next

Thanksgiving one fifty-thousand-dollar nugget to Ellen and another to Miss Minna here, and we will drink your health in a cup of Mrs. Odonto's best black coffee."

Poor Mr. Perry knew this, of course, well nigh as well as Fergus; only the sinews of war failed him. Here Fergus came to the rescue. He had a square talk with Perry and learned his whole story. Perry had broken down in Swansea and "was cleaned out" there, as the carnal say. What was the break-down I do not know. Only it was not dishonesty and it was not gambling. Probably it was liquor, which is at the bottom of so large a proportion of the wretchedness of our times that, when you know nothing to the contrary, you may take this for granted. Whatever it was, Fergus knew. I do not. Fergus had confidence enough in his man to believe him a man of honor; and after consulting with Ellen and with her full consent, Fergus borrowed at the First National Bank five hundred dollars on the pledge of bonds to that amount, and boldly lent the money to Mr. Perry to go to Arizona, to try his fortune. He got letters for him to General Fremont, to Mrs. Fremont, and to Mr. Weber, and before Christmas Mr. Perry was on his way.

And this adventure went much farther than they supposed. Letters came from Mr. Perry every week. Sometimes he was up; sometimes he was down. But one May morning, just after Fergus had hung a basket of arbutus, of liverwort, and anemone on the handle of Ellen's door, he walked down to the village for his mail, and in the mail was the critical letter from San Xavier del Bac on which hinges the end of this story.

Mr. Perry had obtained control of just the property he wanted. Capital was needed, of course; but capital would come, could one be sure of brains, scientific knowledge, and business faculty. As for the sinking of shafts, the development of the mine, and the other general work of bringing the one to be fit for anything, Mr. Perry had no fear for his own ability. But as for the smelting, he was wholly dissatisfied with all he saw—as well with the old Mexican traditions as with the new hand-to-mouth California makeshifts, as he coolly called them. And the letter, therefore, ended with these pregnant sentences : " In short, my dear sir, you have seen my drift already. If you could come out here to live—of course, with your wife—I believe we could have the best mine here and the best *smelting mills.* And, observe, the last is vastly the more important of the two. A mine may or may not play out ; or there may be a thousand better mines. *Quien sabe ?* But there cannot be better smelting than you and I ought to be able to establish here. Then let there be a thousand and one mines, why, so much the better for you and me.

" Could not Miss Ville-Fosse send for one of those brothers of hers from Freiberg ? I do not want to underrate your chemistry, nor my own, of course ; but I observe that the German gentlemen here are reticent, and that some things which they do they do in secret. If you and I were together, and Mr. Ville-Fosse prove to have the average practical knowledge of the Freiberg people I have known here and in Europe, why, we would beat the world."

IV. ANOTHER DINNER.

It was on the strength of this letter that Fergus himself went to Arizona, to see how the country lay. A costly journey it was, too, for Arizona was a hard place to reach in those days, nor is it easy to reach now. But Fergus persuaded Rising, at the *New Altona* newspaper office, that he wanted some letters from the mines; and, on the strength of an engagement there, he made another engagement with a great "Metropolitan Daily" to write to them. And, by living on light fare as he travelled, and writing on these letters at every instant when trains ceased joggling, he made both ends meet without too terrible an inroad on the little capital, which would be so essential if Perry's views were confirmed.

And Perry's views were confirmed, so far that Fergus came back to New Padua, and persuaded Ellen Markley to marry him then and there. If he went to Arizona, she would go. And he went, and she went. Fritz Ville-Fosse had been written to, and he was only too glad to see in place with his own eyes ores which he had written about and heard about for so many years. He was even able, with the help of his friends, to contribute something to the little capital of the trio; while Fergus was doing his utmost, by way of wedding preparations, to induce his friends also to subscribe—for their own good, as he believed.

So is it that the next Thanksgiving day finds Mr. and Mrs. Menet—that is to say, Fergus and his wife Ellen—keeping house in their adobe palace, within the sound of the bells of the old mission church of Santa Madre de los Remedios. And these bells, which men said were two centuries old, were ringing all that morning. Mr. Perry, who was a guest, said that it was St. Jonathan's day; but this was his little joke. He had been out with his gun two or three days before, and had brought in two matchless turkeys for the feast;

and while in every adobe in the neighborhood Mexican women were at work over their *ollas* or were frying their *tortillas*, Ellen and Minna Ville-Fosse found themselves recalling the memories of Mrs. Odonto's kitchen, as they rolled out pastry, stewed the great dice they cut from majestic pumpkins, and performed other rites of the annual mysteries of New England.

Mr. Perry could not be made to go with Fergus to attend at mass, at the daily service of the church of Santa Madre. Not he! He would watch those stupid dogs who were building the chimney. But Fergus was true, not so much to a conviction, indeed, as to a sentiment; and, with devotion quickened by gratitude, and gratitude more grateful for devotion, joined the queer company of dirty children, and mothers as dirty, who kneeled before the broken altar-rail, as a swarthy priest, in vestments of the most equivocal character, elevated the host and repeated what he could from a liturgy which he could not understand. Shall we blame Fergus if the prayer that he uttered in his heart of hearts was accompanied by the vow that these mothers and these children should have better chances in the future to come into a reasonable service to a loving Father?

The elevation of the host did Fergus no harm, to be sure. The hour he spent in the old church was an hour which watered and sunned seeds which will yet bear good harvest. At last he left the odor of incense and other smells, of garlic and of onions, which incense had not smothered, and came out into the sweet, open air, and stood on the great slab in front of the church, to give thanks again for air, and sunlight, and blue sky, and health, and wife, and home. As he looked right and left, he saw the crowd of loafers, "greasers," and dogs which announced the arrival of a stranger. He was not so far beyond the realm of curiosity but that he walked toward the crowd, while a morose man would have walked away from it. Two horsemen appeared, as they might have done in one of Mr. James's novels; and behind them quite a little train of *burros*—good, patient creatures, with their packs. A horde of Mexican children surrounded the party.

The leading horseman touched his hat to Fergus, who advanced cordially to offer him the hospitalities of the village.

"Can you be so kind as to point to us the way to the mines of Mr. Perry or Mr. Menet?"

"I am Mr. Menet," said Fergus, hastily. And then light struck him; and he saw—what the quicker reader has discovered already—that here was Fritz Ville-Fosse in person. Warm was the greeting, eager the surprise, unintelligible the explanations why his letters had not come in advance; and cheerily did Fergus lead him to the adobe, where they surprised Ellen and Minna, even as they were dishing up the Thanksgiving dinner.

Many a dinner had these six afterward in that adobe house—now on the fat of the land, now on minced meat made from the dinner of the day before, and now on *tortillas* and hard tack, as might be ordered for them in the providence of the good God; but never was there breakfast, luncheon, dinner, tea, or supper (for the house was carried on on the five-meal principle), never was a crust broken in the daily sacrament of a common meal, but that first Thanksgiving day was remembered, and the memory carried a blessing. That Fritz should actually come in upon Minna when her hands upheld a gigantic chicken-pie ; that she had courage and persistency enough not to drop it, in her wonder and delight ; that feast, and not famine, should be his welcome—all this, and all that belonged to it, made the first Thanksgiving at Santa Madre a feast to be long remembered.

They talked and they talked—now in good English and broken German, now in good German and broken English—till the small hours came in. And in that talk were laid the foundations which, in all the doubts and difficulties of years, secured ultimate triumph. That famous firm of Menet, Perry, and Ville-Fosse was then formed. That famous monogram, which unites the M., P. and V.—a monogram so familiar to those who have handled the Santa Madre ingots—was then and there devised. Minna's was the pattern which out of a dozen commanded every suffrage ; nor has it ever been changed in their years of prosperity, more than fabulous.

And it has been prosperity well deserved. In all these years, whether of struggle or of success, whether of adversity or of prosperity, they have held to the cordiality of the first Thanksgiving dinners. Each of the men has the word " Together" cut upon his watch-seal. Each of the women has " Together" inscribed on the inner surface of her wedding-ring. Ellen has known the times when she said that, as shoemakers' wives are ill-shod, the wives of smelters are short of money. Ellen has rocked one baby with her foot on the cradle, has penned up another with two chairs on their sides, while she fried the *tortillas* which were the only dinner, because her oven was so full of silver-bricks, which were hidden in it, that she could not use it for her weekly baking. That was in the week when they had had the riot just below them, at the Sweetwater Gulch ; and when their own priest was drunk, and nobody knew in the morning what might happen before night. But in all such trials, as in the trials of prosperity, so much harder to be borne, those five have always held "together."

V. PARIS.

And now, as it happens, the last Thanksgiving of this story is in Paris.

Fergus had been invited, in a very civil letter from the president of the Bank of France, to one more conference on this knotty question, whether *argent* shall continue to be *l'argent*. Shall silver be money? Of course, as one of the men through whose hands an immense fraction of it passes every year, his opinion for the present and his judgment for the future must be taken.

Fergus had telegraphed to his agent in Paris as to his wishes for a home for the winter, and the agent had bought the grand old Hotel De Rosny, with the pictures—oh ! such pictures—and the furniture. And to this pleasant home he and Ellen and the children and the nurses had gone direct from the train ; and they felt as much at home as in New Padua, at Mrs. Odonto's. The children might well say this, as they had never seen that paradise. And Ellen had brought out with her dear old Mrs. Weeks, who could, with some effort, concoct as good a squash pie in the elaborate cuisine of the Hotel De Rosny as Ellen herself had made in Mrs. Odonto's kitchen.

"Only," said Fergus, gallantly, "it has not exactly the finish and the flavor."

"Who do you think is coming?" said he, as he ran

in on Wednesday evening. "Perry and his wife have just landed at Brest. The Pereire has had a wonderful trip. They have taken the night train, so as to be with us to-morrow morning."

"And to-morrow is Thanksgiving day!" cried Ellen. "Mrs. Weeks and I have contrived everything as if we were at home. Turkeys, chicken-pies, Marlboro' puddings, cranberry tarts, Washington pies, nuts, figs, and raisins—you shall not know you are not in South Slickville."

And Fergus said: "As soon as I heard that Minna would be here, I telegraphed for Fritz. Here is his answer. He could not arrive on the regular mail-train; but he has chartered a special engine and is crossing from Saxony, a hundred kilometres an hour, at this living moment, to be with you at breakfast-time to-morrow. He does not say, but I hope his little wife is with him."

And his little wife was with him; and Minna—for the reader sees that Minna is Mrs. Perry—Minna and her husband and that big Ralph were, happily, at the Hotel De Rosny at nine o'clock. And there she met her blushing new sister; and the big, red-faced, red-whiskered Fritz stood behind the door, and caught his sister and almost crushed her in his arms. This time he surprised her as much as she had surprised him at Santa Madre.

As they sat, after dinner, just these six, after going back over every queer experience of that wild life of Santa Madre, and of San Xavier, and Guaymas, and memories of old Father Kino and the rest, Fergus said: "I dined with a queer set yesterday. It was at the minister's—minister of finance, you know. We had this young Rothschild and Monte Cristo's son (who is a quiet, well-informed fellow ; speaks English as well as you do), one of Van Beest's people, the president of the Bank of England, and the president of the Bank of France—only we seven and the three ladies of the house. It was charming to see how they cut the shop. You would not have known that there was a silver dollar or a gold napoleon in the world. On the other hand, we almost pretended that the minister had dug the potatoes with his own hand ; that Madame had milked the cows and made the butter ; that Rothschild had been a-fishing and brought in the dorado ; and that Mademoiselle — what is her name? — had cooked the whole. We were Arcadian in our simplicity.

"But, as we talked after dinner, we all drew up round the fire—just as if we had been in England or at home—and Mlle. Clara drew out young Monte Cristo very prettily. You see there were not too many of us to talk across the fireplace and all to join. You will guess that the general talk hushed, by one of the spells that fall sometimes, when he said :

"'Oh, my father's love for the dear Abbé passed the love of angels for each other.'

"'Why,' cried Ellen, ' the Abbé was the man in the Chateau d'If who taught Monte Cristo language and told him where the diamonds were.'

"'Yes,' said Fergus. 'We were all still as mice to hear young Monte Cristo say : " Every step of my father's prosperity afterward followed on that love of his for the dear Abbé and of the Abbé for him. My father was a hard hater ; but when he died he said to me : ' Remember that the secret of success is love.' That is my motto, Mademoiselle," he said, and that with no nonsense in his tone.'

"The girl apprehended his mood, saw that he would

prefer to be silent, and turned to young Rothschild. 'And what do you say, M. le Baron?' said she. 'What pretty story can you tell us to teach us the secret of success?'

"'My story is very easily told,' said he. 'It is the one tradition of our house. Rothschild Brothers is Rothschild Brothers because the brothers of the old firm lived like brothers. They had no separate accounts. Each man lived for the whole. When you have asked all your questions, Mademoiselle, I will tell you a little story of the early days.'

"'And you, Mr. Newland?' said the girl, laughing, and turning to the president of the Bank of England.

"'Oh,' said he, 'you must ask our friend here if he ever failed us when we needed him.' And then, with his English pride, he added: 'Or if we ever failed him.' He turned to the old gray-haired president of the Bank of France; and he smiled and bowed assent, well pleased, indeed, with all the dignity of the old *régime*.

"The thing was growing serious. These gentlemen took it *au serieux*, indeed. But the girl did not blench.

"'And you, Mr. Van Beest—what do they say in Holland?'

"'They say, Mademoiselle, that if a furlong of the dike gives way half a state is deluged. But they say that when every yard of the dike is riveted in with every other yard, we defy ocean itself. Mademoiselle, it is the infinite of the spirit against the infinite of the waves.'

"The girl was serious now; but she had begun her catechism, and she would finish it. So she turned to me.

"'M. Menet,' she said, 'what commands success in America?'

"I pressed my seal ring so, just above the 'line of life' on her hand, upon the plump white ball below her thumb, and I said :

"'Mademoiselle, if you could see what I have printed on your hand, you would read the word "TOGETHER."'"

"Do you tell me," said the excited Mrs. Fréchette, almost screaming and dropping a brushful of cobalt blue full on the high light of a snow-drift in her drawing, "do you tell me that this man in a buffalo coat, who lifted Miss Bourn so easily, is the great bonanza man?"

"No ; the great bonanza man came after him. He is the one with a red silk handkerchief round his throat. I do not know the name of the forward man."

But at this moment the front door of the palace opened, and Hector Van Sandfoord appeared, followed by Mr. Menet and Mr. Decker, whom he introduced to the ladies.

It required all Mrs. Fréchette's promptness to receive them as if she had been discussing colors or politics or religion the instant before, and had not been reading the biography of one of them. As for Mary Van Sandfoord, she simply bowed as the gentlemen were presented, and Theodora, as an invalid, might be permitted to be a little flushed. Mrs. Hackmatack, who was really the least guilty of the party, hoped nobody would notice her, and, in truth, no one did.

"Do not let us break up your reading," said Mr. Menet, after Cæsar had placed two light chairs for them in the passage-way. And he actually put out his hand for the guilty story, which was still lying on Mary's open bag.

But, with that infinite promptness of woman's guilt, Mary was beforehand with him.

"No," she said, as she laid back the paper in the bag, and drew out a little volume of H. H.'s essays. "It was only a little Thanksgiving story I was showing to Mrs. Fréchette. Do you rememer Helen Hunt's account of her first passage through the mountains?"

Guilty Mary Van Sandfoord, and wise as the serpent who first tempted her kind!

Mr. Menet did not remember; but he was glad if they had heart to talk about Thanksgiving. Were they not afraid that they should lose their Christmas?

CHAPTER III.

SNOW-BOUND—NAHUM BARROW'S REVENGE.

AND so came to the ladies the full announcement of what had been clear enough to the men long before, but what had not been formally proclaimed in the palace, in the confusion of the loss and the rescue. With this long detention, now counting seven or eight hours, there was no chance whatever of reaching Council Bluffs at four o'clock on Christmas eve, or the afternoon of Christmas eve, as the schedule time proposed. Lucky, indeed, if they were at Council Bluffs at midnight.

Still, Mary Van Sandfoord was clear that they could run out by a morning train to Hastings, and that the Corneaus would meet them at the station.

Hopeful Mary!

As for Theodora Bourn, she was more indifferent to the Corneaus.

The through passengers in a well-arranged Pullman grow to a feeling of possession in it, akin to the feeling of a passenger on a well-arranged White Star packet. One is more at home with Cæsar or with John, the porter, than he is with the bumptious or the ignorant waiter at the Hag-daggery-dag Hotel, whom he never saw before, and never will see again. The Corneaus's house was not the Hag-daggery-dag Hotel, but it was a new place for poor Theodora. It meant one more set of new faces to be seen, new names to be learned, and the girl had had—oh, so much of that experience in this last year, that she shrank from it. While in the palace, she knew where she was, and could call it, if she chose, her home.

At this moment, too, Mr. Decker at her side, having made every inquiry about her health, and having been thanked most prettily for his help, was boldly and skilfully turning the subject from the accident and rescue, as if it were the most insignificant affair. He caught at the hint which the word "Thanksgiving" gave, and made some absurd story of the effort he, with some friends he had visited on a ranch, had made for a Thanksgiving dinner. The story was nothing, but it was enough to laugh at, and drew from Theodora some little experience in housekeeping on the actual shore of the Pacific. In that region she had seen more than he—indeed, he said, laughing, that he was only an in-doors miner—that he knew his pots and crucibles and agents and re-agents better than he did the trees and the mountains. "A laboratory, alas, is much the same in Arizona as in Freiberg, Miss Bourn."

"You will never persuade me that you are any carpet knight," said Theodora frankly. "At least you can wear snow-shoes."

"Oh, as to that, it is the accomplishment of a gentleman in some countries.

"At the finest dinner-party I ever saw there was an English officer of rank, who was telling us most curious things about Hudson's Bay and the northern Rockies. He said he had crossed from the Atlantic to the Pacific at one time and another. Some man asked him how he went, and he said : ' I walked.'

" Really, Miss Bourn, that man had walked, and, most of the way, on snow-shoes. And I have seen ladies walk on snow-shoes too, and they walked very prettily and very well."

"I will have a pair," said Theodora, "before I go after my veil again."

"Are you a New Englander?" asked he, determined again to get off the adventure of the morning.

"My mother was. My father was from the West India Islands. But we always kept Thanksgiving, as I tell you."

"I am a regular Down-Easter. I came from where they jump off. We have a capital Thanksgiving story of the Revolution in our family;" and he was going to open on the story, when Theodora said:

"No, Mr. Decker, if there is a story to tell, it is common property." And turning to the others she said: "Mr. Decker is going to tell us all a Thanksgiving story of the Revolution."

Now, the truth was that Mr. Decker would greatly have preferred to talk to Miss Theodora alone. But he was a gentleman, and when he found the turn things had taken, he said he would rather not try to tell the story. A kinsman of his had written it out, and, as it happened, he had it in a pocket of his overcoat. He produced an envelope somewhat thumbed, took from it a scrap of newspaper, and read them the story of

NAHUM BARROW'S REVENGE.

A THANKSGIVING TALE.

NAHUM BARROW was on his way north, through Virginia, with private despatches from General Greene to Washington, at the headquarters of the army. He had pressed the horse he rode rather faster than the result justified; and when, late on Wednesday night, he rode into the home-inclosures of the plantation, of which, for an hour, he had watched the smoke, he was glad to believe that so generous an establishment would have a professed blacksmith among its slaves, for the mare had been going on three shoes all the afternoon, and, for the last hour, one of them had disappeared. The sun had fairly set by the time Nahum and the mare arrived at the house itself. A sort of sedateness hung over the place, which Nahum found it hard to explain to himself ; nor was there the noisy and eager gathering of the clans which he was used to now in his Virginian experiences. But this reticence was explained, after he had knocked at the door, by the appearance of the host on whose comfortable quarters Nahum had billeted himself ; for, as Nahum saw in a moment, this was one of the Society of Friends. A tall man, of severe but yet benevolent enough face, held a candle above his head, to see what manner of man it was who knocked so freely.

Nahum asked if he could receive a night's hospitality, which was readily granted. He dismounted, and asked his friend's advice about the mare. A lantern was brought, for it need not be said that the candle had been immediately extinguished by the wind. The examination which followed showed not only that she had but two shoes, but, which Nahum had not known, that one of her legs was bleeding.

"Got into a hole with her in the corduroy, where the wood-road comes in," said Nahum. "It's half an hour back ; but the old critter scrabbled out so spry that she didn't give me no chance to get off and see if she'd scraped herself."

"I wish there were any road-master," said the other ; " but they do not know what that word means. Nor do they know well what he would do if he were here. Did thee find the road better this side the creek?"

"Fust-rate," said Nahum, guessing rightly that at the creek his Quaker friend's plantation began. And then he followed in a eulogy—true enough, but perhaps a little suspicious—of the neatness of all the arrangements of the farm around him. These eulogies neither deterred nor hastened Reuben Dyer, as he took off the trooper's saddle-bags and his saddle; as he led the mare to water, which she refused; and as, with such appliances as the well-furnished stable afforded, he washed and dressed the wounded leg. In all these offices Nahum attempted to do his full share; but his host construed a host's duties in the largest sense. He hardly permitted Nahum's presence, as he himself attended to the mare, and even rubbed her down with his own hands. Two tall negro boys stood by, admiring; but, excepting to hold the lanterns and once and again to do an errand, they left the mare's business in their master's hands.

After half an hour of such careful work, it was clear enough that nothing more could be done for the poor beast, and Nahum and his host returned to the house.

In the midst of the decorous reticence of the household and an occasional formal statement which indicated a theoretical dislike of the profession of arms, the trooper soon saw that his presence was not disagreeable. He was a little tempted to play with the professed pacific habit of the household, to affect that there was no war, and to hang up his sword on the wooden pin in the wall, as he might hang up a riding-whip. If they did not want to know where Greene had come to, why should he tell them? If they were willing to take the chances of Cornwallis's raiding through their farms, and Tarleton's driving off their horses, and the swift *commissariat* of both at work in killing their cattle, why should Nahum Barrow care? He could talk about Virginia fences, as contrasted with stone walls ; or he could discuss the points of a Durham bull ; he could give an opinion as to the price of tobacco ; nay, if need were, he could hold his tongue. Quakers can be reticent when there is need ; but a Connecticut boy of twenty-three, bred under the traditions of the grumpy silence of Uncas and his Pequots, can be as mum as the best of them, if he feel necessity.

But such fell resolutions of telling no war stories melted away beneath the genial kindness of the motherly head of the household ; beneath the modest smiles of a certain pretty Martha, who gave her personal attention to the waffles which crowned the feast which awaited Nahum ; and beneath the rapturous admiration of Thomas and Elnathan, two fine boys, who could scarcely keep their well-bred hands off the trooper's haversack, and occasionally retired into the hall, to worship the sabre which hung there, with such admiring glances as the Ashantee fanatic is supposed to bestow upon his fetish. These traits of consideration disarmed Nahum, and as the generous Bohea entered into the machinery of his system and quickened his life ; as his hunger appeased itself after one and another charge upon the " chicken fixings" which had been placed before him ; when, with a fresh fork and knife he advanced to deal with the waffles, in their turn, he opened freely, as a lonely soldier should, upon the war and its history and its future. He fought Monmouth over again ; he detailed with humor even the critical passages in his own experiences at Hotham's

Neck; he explained, as far as a prudent subaltern might, the resources on which Greene must rely.; and he digressed, with what he thought excusable exaggeration, upon the matchless resources of Cornwallis and Tarleton. Of these last he knew, in truth, as little as this reader, and that is saying a good deal; but, with the wisdom of a serpent, Nahum said to himself: "Ef these people aren't a little skeered, they won't give the General any supplies. Little enough he gets from them now." Supposing, incorrectly, that his laudable end would justify his unworthy means, the soldier, therefore, dashed into statements as to Cornwallis and his forces for which he was largely indebted to his imagination.

The evening passed pleasantly in this exciting talk, and it was an hour later than usual when all parties went to bed.

The next morning brought another sight at Reuben Dyer's plantation. The wind had come round to the northwest, and at the earliest dawn there was already half an inch of snow on the fields, and the trees were taking on the most grotesque forms. At breakfast-time snow was still falling. Nor had the diagnosis of the mare's leg proved favorable. Reuben Dyer had expressed his readiness to shoe her, and the trooper had yielded to Reuben's superior knowledge of farriery; but the poor creature limped so sadly when she was led to water that it seemed cruel to take her out on roads so far snow-covered that she could not see where her feet would fall.

"If thy errand requires haste," said Reuben, "thee shall be made welcome to either of my horses; but they are more fit for draught than for fast riding. My pacer, of which the boy Elnathan spake to thee, is, as he told thee, at Alexandria."

Nahum had himself taken a surreptitious look at the horses, and, while he respected their good points, had concluded that he could make better time in forty-eight hours on his own feet than on theirs. He reserved his decision, however, till a certain Mike Slaughter, who was the authority on the subject of horses' ailments, could be consulted. Doctor or quack, he should determine whether the mare could or could not go on. As the day passed, Nahum determined that he should make the best speed by accepting the Quaker's hospitable invitation, and spending another night. When he announced this decision, however, he received a severe wound from his hostess.

"Mr. Dyer wants me to stay the night," said Nahum cheerily to her, as he entered her kitchen; "'n' I guess I will. It's Thanksgivin' day, 'n' I don't want to travel, ef the country's service don't require it. We'll keep our Thanksgivin' together, Miss Marthy."

"Keep what?" said the pretty girl, startled.

"Keep Thanksgivin'!" said the astonished Nahum, with his eyes opened. "Ain't your meetin' open?"

"There are so few Friends in the county," said Prudence Dyer, Martha's mother, who stepped to the fore, "that we have no regular meeting on Fifth Day, nor, indeed, on First Day, unless some Friend pass in travel."

"But you keep Thanksgivin' day?" persisted the trooper.

The woman stared as her daughter had done. It soon appeared that she had no more idea than Martha had of what he was talking about. Nahum drew from his inner pocket a well-worn copy of the Connecticut

Courant. He pointed to them Governor Trumbull's "Proclamation for a day of Public Thanksgiving and Praise." "Ef I was down to Tolland," said he, "I should be jest now goin' to meetin'. 'N' the girls, Miss Marthy, would be steppin' round spry, with the chickens and the old gobbler, I tell you. They's only one thing missin' there to-day ; you be sure of that." And to Martha's inquiring look, with a broken voice, not wholly soldierly, he said : "The old man would have a better time ef I looked in on um jest as they was fittin' off f' meet'n'."

The women stopped in their work and listened with as much curiosity as they would have done had Lady Mary Wortley Montagu described to them a dance of wild dervishes ; but Nahum's rather voluble narrative was broken by Reuben Dyer's entrance. He heard the young man to the end of his eager home memories, and then said :

"We have neither time nor disposition for such fooleries, young man. If the Almighty God had wished these observances, he would not leave the announcement to the civil magistrates. He hath simpler methods of proclaiming His will than the newspapers. Prudence," he continued, "we will keep thy goose for another day's dinner. There is enough left of the hominy and pork for to-day. Young man," he added, with a certain asperity which Nahum had not observed before, "if thee wishes to see Michael Slaughter, he is coming down the hill."

Nahum understood very well that he was in no position to discuss matters with his host ; but one consequence of this little passage at arms was that he pronounced the mare's leg good for ten miles, if he rode her with care, and left his hosts with a cordial enough good-by, while he had two hours of daylight before him.

It was more than a year before Nahum Barrow met his Friendly hosts again. I will not say that he did not sometimes think of that pretty and deft little Martha ; I will not say that the quiet little Quakeress did not sometimes think of him ; but the reader of this reminiscence of a hundred years ago must not build too much on those expressions of mine. Spring and summer passed. Cornwallis came up as near as Hanover Court-House, and Reuben Dyer recognized that fact so far that he had four cows driven into a fastness in the wilderness, and that, at dead of night, he buried with his own hands a box which held forty or fifty joes and a hundred Spanish dollars and six silver teaspoons. Then Cornwallis went back to James River, and the spoons were dug up again and the cattle came back from the swamp. The crops were all well in at last, the harder duties of harvest were finished, and on a lovely afternoon, at the very end of St. Martin's summer, our pretty Martha and her mother, Prudence (scarcely less charming), were standing on the broad step, watching the glories of the west, as the sun sank rapidly behind the Blue Ridge. Reuben would not have confessed that the glory of sunset had lured him from his work. All the same it had. The women would have confessed this for themselves. Nor would it have hurt Reuben to confess it.

Of a sudden the well-remembered mare clattered up the roadway at a hard gallop, guided by the well-remembered Nahum. My pretty Martha fairly blushed, so provoked was she because she was thinking of him before he came, and so she looked prettier than ever. The handsome trooper gave his hand cordially to each of them, and then was off the saddle in a moment. He had come, he said, with the compliments of Major Rice and Colonel Huntington, of the Fourth Connecticut Brigade, who were about an hour behind him. If it were not disagreeable to Friend Dyer, they would be pleased if the brigade might bivouac for the night upon the pasture which Nahum remembered by the corn-barn. Reuben Dyer might be sure that the men would be careful, and would ask for nothing but water, and would burn nothing but brush.

Joy leaped to Martha's eyes. At last she should see an army, or a part of an army—she who had never seen any soldier but Nahum Barrow. Indeed, a calm cheerfulness stole over the face of Prudence; and Reuben himself showed all the cordiality of a Virginian and all the hospitality of a Friend, as he returned his manly answer :

"Say to thy friends that we are glad they have chosen this road."

Nahum did not whisper that it was he who had chosen the road and suggested it to Colonel Huntington.

"If thee will sleep thyself in the room thee had last year, thee can bring as many of thy friends as thee chooses. In the rest of the house Prudence and Martha made beds for the twenty-three Friends when the yearly meeting was last here, and they can do the same now. Then there is the stable, and the old stable that thee has not seen, and the corn-bins, and William Waylen's tobacco-shed. As for water, the boys shall draw some casks for thy friends, so that they need not go to the creek; but as thee says the men are prudent, I will bid Jotham haul a cask of cider also to the pasture before they come. The night may be cold."

Nahum was well pleased that he had not miscalculated his friends' hospitality. He thanked them cordially, said he should soon return, and rode back with his tidings. Martha and Prudence, with the help of the boy, Archippus, sprang to their task, if one may use a healthy piece of the vernacular. Reuben called Jotham, and the two rolled a generous cask of cider upon a drag, and placed it upon skids convenient, just where they took down two lengths of Virginia fence for the entrance of the soldiers into their camp-ground. They were placing two large casks of water on the skids when a large party of horsemen, well mounted, rode up to the house, guided by Nahum. These were Colonel Huntington, with the gentlemen of his personal staff, and, indeed, almost all the staff-officers of the brigade. The more studied courtesies of the camp mingled charmingly with the inborn courtesy of Quaker life. These polished gentlemen showed their hosts in a hundred ways how grateful they were for a reception so cordial. On the other hand, without saying so in words, Reuben's family found as many ways to show that, in spite of their disapproval of war, they were glad Cornwallis was a prisoner and thankful to the gallant men who had arrested his career.

Early the next morning, as the pearly gray of the sky showed that a perfect day was before them, Colonel Huntington waited on Reuben Dyer, whom he found at his wood-pile, directing the loading of a cord or two of wood, which he was sending off to the regimental camp-fire.

"The men may not have the tools or the time to cut it," he said to the colonel.

The colonel thanked him, and then said that he

and all his officers were most grateful for these courtesies. Would it be presuming too much if they availed themselves of such perfect weather and of the neighborhood of such friends, and permitted the men to rest themselves all day? Their march had been rapid till now, and he did not care to have the men spend more time than the Sabbath itself at Alexandria.

"Thee can easily reach Alexandria by Seventh-Day evening, if thee does not march till to-morrow morning," said the Quaker, promptly, almost eagerly. "Let the poor fellows stay; let them stay. I am only sorry we have not barns as big as thee will find in Lancaster," he said, remembering fondly the farming of his boyhood.

"One thing more," said the courtly colonel, "for you have learned before this in life that beggars are apt to be choosers. Would thy friend, Waylen, in whose tobacco-shed the boys of my own regiment have been snoring so loudly—would he object to have some of them hold a meeting there this morning? One of the officers is moved to address the men on the manifold exhibitions of Divine goodness in this surrender; but he will rather speak to them in the woods than offend friends so kindly."

"William Waylen object to a fifth-day meeting, if I call one?" This was the first exclamation of Reuben; but in an instant he controlled the rising flame. In language more decorous he said that he knew his neighbor, and all his family would wish to be present, and that he should send one of his negro boys to the neighboring houses and notify all.

"Ask that the poor blacks may come themselves, also," said Colonel Huntington, and there was enough in his intonation to show Reuben Dyer that he and his guest were at one in their notions about these people.

Thus simply was it settled that the old tobacco-shed, which for years had not been used for the purpose it was built for, should be this day a crowded temple. At ten o'clock, to the delight, scarcely disguised, of Martha, the different regiments, in their best holiday trim, marched by the house in order. For the first time in her life, she heard a band of military music. Governor Hazen's brigade band, in the intimacies of the weeks since Yorktown, had picked up from a Hessian band-master the music from the march in "Judas Maccabæus," and for the first time this girl knew the wonders of Handel. Neither she nor her mother knew what was meant by the elegance of a marching salute, as the regiments passed the door ; but it seemed to Martha hardly the same world as that which had moved by so quietly only the day before. In the chaise, which had been made ready by Jotham, she and her mother followed to the improvised meeting-house, and there they took the places reserved for them in the midst of the great assembly. She saw that there was more than one elder on the bench which fronted them. She heard a thousand voices join in singing :

"Be Thou, O God, exalted high !"

Her whole heart was with the eager, pale young man who, in prayer, praised God for such marvellous blessings as seemed opening on the country. The most glowing language of the Book of Revelation and of the Psalms of David was none too high for his thankfulness nor for hers, and she felt that the "goodness, new every morning and fresh every evening," was the only adequate explanation of the blessedness which had come to hearts which for years had been bowed down in anxiety, or to homes like hers, now just set free from the fear of sword and fire.

A taller and older man then rose to address them; not at great length (the army had cured them all of long speeches), but with a crisp, sharp, dry manner of speech, yet quite unlike the preachers whom Martha had heard at quarterly meetings. "He hath made of a city a heap; of a defenced city a ruin; a palace of strangers to be no city. It shall never be built." He began with these words, sharply emphasized. He did not condescend to say where they came from; but Martha could see that Colonel Huntington, in a Bible he held in his hand, turned quickly to the place and smiled his approval of the selection. With free disregard of Jerusalem, or of Samaria, or of any Eastern city, the speaker led his hearers at once to that fenced city of Yorktown which the Lord had just destroyed by their enginery. The death of Scammell, whom these boys adored; the storm of the two redoubts; the waving of the handkerchief of surrender; the stately march of the final ceremony—all were described in language half of New England and half from the Hebrew texts. The men listened eagerly, with their mouths half open and with eyes fixed upon him. When he closed, crying out in a rapturous outburst, "To Thee, the Lord of Hosts, in whose might kings reign and nations are born, to Thee and to thy great name be all the glory and all the praise," Colonel Huntington and more than one of those around him broke out, unconsciously even, into ejaculations of "Amen."

As the meeting broke up, a tall Virginian, standing on a large stump in the roadway, invited all who were present to join in a barbecue, which he said had been suddenly arranged in the edge of a grove close at hand. "Three good porkers," said he, "and as handsome a steer as there is in Fairfax County has been roasting there since daybreak. Nothing's too good for them as scotched my Lord Cornwallis."

"The ranks of Tuscany" did not forget to cheer when this announcement was made. Colonel Huntington nodded to the gentlemen of his staff, and they ran to the line officers to give the general's permission.

Reuben was fearful, when he saw this, that his plans might be broken in upon, and said hastily:

"No, no, friend Huntington, this is not for thee and for these" (gentlemen, he would have said, but that the memories of George Fox forbade) "for these friends. If thee will dine at our house, thee will see that we have made ready. Friend Meadows will be there and Elizabeth Meadows, Friend Wingfield also, and Mary Wingfield, and some other Friends."

It was clear enough that the barbecue was for the men, and some other provision for the staff.

And so it shortly proved. In the absence of the worshippers at the tobacco-shed, long tables had been set in the hall, in the kitchen, in the sitting-room, and in the "best room" of Friend Dyer's house. They ran transversely from corner to corner, so as to give the utmost possible room for those who served the feast. Indeed, there was no room in the house where the brilliant staff and the line officers could assemble, and they stood chatting in front, under the great locust trees, until notice was given that the party in the kitchen had brought across the viands with which the feast was to begin. Then Colonel Huntington was led to the head of one table, Major Fish to the head of another, while Reuben himself sat at the head of a third. For a minute there was a dead-hush silence, as silently each guest asked a blessing, and then the gay company fell to. Prudence, and Martha, and Elizabeth, and Mary, and other Friends of that sex who cannot be named ; Jotham, and Archippus, and I know not how many grinning boys of their color, with Phebe, and Dorcas, and other girls as black as they, passed from the kitchen to the tables and back again, and with one and another dainty, in which Virginian cookery and Quaker science were combined, supplied the festival. Haunches of venison, and great turkeys from the forest, and ducks and chickens and geese from the poultry-yard, with every curious variety of pastry and of preserve, had been brought in from ten miles around. Nahum Barrow found his place near the foot of his colonel's table. It had been intimated to him that all parties would be more at ease if he remained at the homestead and did not join in the barbecue, and Nahum had his own reasons for complying.

It must be confessed that the customs of that age were not the customs of this. It soon proved that the additional casks of cider, which had been sent to the barbecue, had not exhausted Reuben Dyer's store ; and Major Fish and Colonel Antill, claiming the privileges of billeted officers, had sent their orderlies to the wagon-master, with orders for some Port and Madeira, which had been discovered in Cornwallis's pillage collected at Yorktown. But the occasion needed no wine for its merriment. Home was before them all. Peace had come after war. Here were men who were to see children who had been born since they left their firesides. All were men who had done the thing they resolved to do. The skies were bright, the future was fair. They were happy and they meant to be.

It was taken for granted that Reuben's prejudices would yield so far that they might drink a few toasts, and, with exuberant enthusiasm, "the Honorable Congress," "His Excellency the Commander-in Chief," "His Most Christian Majesty King Louis," were toasted in their turn. It was after the clapping of hands subsided, which followed a little speech made by Lieutenant de Ménonville, in very funny, broken English, by way of acknowledging the compliment to his sovereign, that Colonel Huntington called to Nahum, at the other end of the table. Through the large doors into the generous hall, the party at the hall table could see and hear the whole.

"Sergeant Barrow," said he, "was there nothing in the *Courant* I handed you which our friends would be glad to hear?"

They all knew that the colonel had received a despatch from the North while they were in the tobaccoshed.

Then Nahum rose to his full height. He was in his best spirits. He held a Connecticut *Courant* so folded that he could read one column with ease.

"BY HIS EXCELLENCY JONATHAN TRUMBULL.

A PROCLAMATION

for a Day of Public Thanksgiving and Praise!

"*Whereas:*

"It hath pleased the Most High God, blessed forever, the Supreme and Righteous Ruler of the World, to answer the Prayers of His People in the Thirteen United States of America by Displays of His Great Might and Unerring Providence, such as no People have deserved, and such as make Nations and Sovereigns bow their Heads in Wonder ; and, *Whereas*, He hath led our Leaders, and taught our Counsellors, and given Courage to our Soldiers, and Victory to our Armies ; and, *Whereas*, He hath watched over the gallant Generals who have led to us from another Continent the loyal Armies of our August Ally ;

"*And, Whereas:* He hath been graciously pleased, in His Constant Mercy, to cause an Abundance of the Fruits of the Earth to be produced for our Sustenance, to give Comfort to our People, and to supply our Armies ; and,

"*Finally and Conspicuously :*

"*Whereas:* He hath been pleased to confound the Counsels of the Foes of Freedom, and to direct that a British general of the first Rank, with his whole Army, should be captured by the Allied Forces under the direction of the American Commander-in-Chief,

" I have, therefore, thought fit, by and with the Advice of the Council, to appoint, and do hereby appoint, Thursday, the eleventh day of December next, to be observed as a day of Thanksgiving and Praise, throughout the State of Connecticut, hereby exhorting our Ministers and People of all Denominations of Christians to observe the same."

Nahum could hardly finish this sentence audibly ; for every Connecticut man, nay, every New England man around him was clapping and cheering, and it is to be feared that but few of them listened very attentively to the directions which followed in the long proclamation as to the subjects of prayer and praise.

But there was silence enough at the end for all to hear again, when Nahum, with his best oratory, made the final proclamation :

" And all Servile Work is forbidden on said Day.

"Given under my hand, in the Council Chamber in New Haven, this 30th day of November, in the sixth year of the Independence of the United States of America, Annoque Domini, 1781.   JONTH. TRUMBULL.

"*God Save the United States of America !*"

The whole party in all the rooms had now gathered together, so that they could hear. With the closing words all cheered, three times three, as Huntington led the cheering; and then forty or fifty voices shouted again: "God save the United States of America!"

The pretty Martha and her charming mother stood behind Reuben, their faces wet with tears, which flowed in the excitement. The staid Reuben himself was standing on his chair, cheering with the most loyal. As he found his feet and the floor again, Major Rice turned to him, and said:

"This is what we call a real Yankee Thanksgiving. How can we thank you enough for giving us Thanksgiving Day in Virginia?"

And as Reuben took the broad hand of the major and grasped it, Nahum Barrow felt that

HE HAD HIS REVENGE.

Paul Decker read with spirit, and there was quite enough of the New England blood in the veins of his hearers to make them heartily applaud Nahum's success in compelling the Virginia Quaker to give a Thanksgiving feast in spite of itself.

It added an element of "human pathos," that he declared that Nahum was his own great-grandfather, or that such was the family tradition.

But reading had already become difficult. For, to the joy of all, the train was again in motion.

The telegraphic line eastward had found its tongue, and the liberated train was again on its way.

So soon as the reading was over, there was a great comparing of watches and time-tables and study of the probable or possible time of arrival at Council Bluffs.

True Americans as they all were, every one took it

for granted that all difficulty was now overcome, that the engine-man would even be able to make up some of the "lost" time, and that, in short, from this moment all would be well.

Theodora declared that she was not going to travel in bed any longer. Cæsar was called, and her great couch was beaten into two sofas. She repaired to the dressing-room, and reappeared carefully refitted, and the party went on no longer as a unit, but in groups of twos and twos.

Fergus Menet talked with the bride; Hector Van Sandfoord kept Mrs. Hackmatack screaming with laughter; George Hackmatack discussed the lines of the spectrum and the compensations of color with Mrs. Fréchette.

And so it happened, as men say, that Paul Decker and Theodora Bourn sat together and talked together.

"Happened!"

As if those three skilful and determined married women, as by foreordination absolute, had not by any fineness of intrigue made it physically impossible that any other combination should be possible.

And yet, after all this designing, there was not one word which Paul Decker said to her, or which she said to him, which might not be displayed in large letters on a newspaper bulletin in Park Row. They talked of California and Arizona; of the beach and the mountains; of cañons and Mount Shasta; of Bret Harte and the *Overland Monthly;* of the best way to press eschscholtzias, so that the moisture should not injure the color as they dried; of the difference between nemophila, as it grows wild, and the great grandchild, nemophila, when it has been transplanted into gardens.

No, dear Mrs. Fréchette, there is not one syllable which you would call sentiment passing between that handsome young man and that timid girl.

I do observe that she does not seem so timid as she did when we called her Black Ribbons, and she was sitting all alone in Number Three.

The early dinner of the train came soon, and the ladies were led carefully back to the dining-room.

Theodora was careful this time, and the moment Mrs. Van Sandfoord took her seat, she sat at her side.

But Mrs. Fréchette was quite equal to such strategy as that.

There seemed no manœuvring. But so it was, that when her four were seated the other side of the passage, Mr. Decker was left standing. There was then no seat left but that next Mrs. Hackmatack, and that brought the young man opposite Miss Bourn, who had been careful that he should not be at her side. So far Mrs. Fréchette was well pleased.

By this time all parties were skilled in the little science of travelling, and now they succeeded in so spinning out the changes of courses, that the dinner should take nearly an hour and a half of the day, which was not yet weary.

Then, as is the custom in palaces, the ladies slept, and the gentlemen retired as if to smoke for an hour.

But at four in the afternoon the ladies had their novels in their hands, and one and another of the gentlemen came back to the palace.

They brought cheerful accounts of the prospect. The road was thought to be open, and, by one rosy account, the train had gained a mile and a half in time.

At the Wild Cat Junction, Menet and Decker had picked up their luggage which had waited for them.

"I have brought you Mrs. Ville-Fosse's sketch-book," he said to Theodora, after he had asked permission to join her. "She trusted it to me to carry to one of her Eastern friends.

"Now, I can show you her studies of my Zuñi friends. See how like this dear old priest is to Dante."

And so they plunged into the luxury of turning over slowly the pages, well-filled with good work, of which each one had some story connected with the events of his really adventurous life in Arizona. For, as Theodora had said of him, Paul Decker was no mere carpet knight. And his exploits, such as they were, really took much wider range than he had pretended, when he spoke of himself as only a man of crucible and blow-pipe. He had voyaged through that deepest cañon of all, where the people have as little knowledge of the upper world as has the poor jackass in a coal-mine. He had hob-a-nobbed with Cochise, and had gone on long scouting parties with the Gray Fox, as the Indians called their true friend, General Crook.

But he never talked of himself. Freshly and simply he told Theodora only of the wonderful things he had seen, or that others had described for him, and left it almost a matter of guess how he came to have seen them or to hear them.

And she found herself so at ease with him that she was explaining things in woodland life which he did not understand. She had been in the open air much more than he had—much more, indeed, than half her waking life—since her babyhood. She knew things in the growth of flowers and shrubs that Decandolle did not know nor Linnæus. Her Indians were not his Apaches, no, indeed, but she could tell him of the half savage, half civil ways of the wretched red-skin stragglers who sometimes came in to barter their forest ware against sugar, in queer little details which lighted up and led along his talk. She forgot herself and he forgot himself in their eager comparing of notes about their experiences of life.

And so it was that talk passed easily on, till it touched even graver things.

He had told her of his descent into the Deep Cañon, and she went back to ask him how he first came into it. He told the story in a very animated way.

CHAPTER IV.

PAUL DECKER'S STORY—HANDS OFF—LULU'S DOLL.

PAUL DECKER'S companions had made a long line of cart-ropes, of lassos, even of sound belts, to the lowest of which he was fastened, as being the lightest of the party, and lowered down, nearly two hundred feet. As he neared the bottom, in an awkward swing to clear a projecting rock the whole line trembled, and about midway parted. Half of it fell on his head; he landed heavily on a pile of the débris from the cliff, and rolled and rolled till he was giddy; but brought up, just conscious, and in time to save his life, on a great bit of rock.

"I can laugh at it now, but I did not laugh then," said he, as he told his story to Miss Bourn.

"No, indeed," cried the eager girl. "Were you not in despair? You had the line, and they—"

"No, I was not in despair. I was on the rack of curiosity. 'What will happen now? What will come next?' I said. Queer, I remembered Sindbad in his dark hole. Don't you remember? And," he paused a little seriously, "to be quite true to you, Miss Bourn, I remembered the yellow dog."

He hardly smiled. He looked almost afraid, as if he had gone too far, yet he looked proud and strong.

Theodora did not in the least understand.

"What *do* you mean, Mr. Decker?"

"Do you not know, really? Then you do not know

what is one of the great comforts of my life. Did you never hear that if a yellow dog had not barked once, this world would not be—that you and I should not be here?"

"No, indeed! How?"

"Why, he was a dog in the Midianites' encampment. You know when they had Joseph as a prisoner, Joseph was escaping in the morning—just as I told you our man Foss got off from Cochise—and the yellow dog barked at him, and Joseph flung a stone at him.

"If Joseph had killed him, why there would never have been corn in Egypt when it was wanted, and you see what would happen.

"Joseph did not hit him. He was taken again, and —well the world is what it is."

"I am glad you tell me this," said Theodora, carefully, and even gratefully. "I think it will make my life easier to me sometimes. Do you say it is written out and printed?"

"I have it in an old *Harper's*," he said. And afterward he found it for her and gave it to her.

It is the story of

HANDS OFF.

I was in another stage of existence. I was free from the limits of Time, and in new relations to Space.

Such is the poverty of the English language that I am obliged to use past tenses in my descriptions. We might have a verb which should have many forms indifferent to time, but we have not.

It happened to me to watch, in this condition, the motions of several thousand solar systems all together. It is fascinating to see all parts of all with equal distinctness—all the more when one has been bothered as much as I have been, in my day, with eye-pieces and object-glasses, with refraction, with prismatic colors and achromatic contrivances. The luxury of having practically no distance, of dispensing with these cumbrous telescopes, and at the same time of having nothing too small for observation, and dispensing with microscopes, fussy if not cumbrous, can hardly be described in a language as physical or material as is ours.

At the moment I describe, I had intentionally limited my observation to some twenty or thirty thousand solar systems, selecting those which had been nearest to me when I was in my schooling on earth. Nothing can be prettier than to see the movement, in perfectly harmonic relations, of planets around their centres, of satellites around planets, of suns, with their planets and satellites, around their centres, and of these in turn around theirs. And to persons who have loved Earth as much as I do, and who, while at school there, have studied other worlds and stars, then distant, as carefully as I have, nothing, as I say, can be more charming than to see at once all this play and interplay; to see comets passing from system to system, warming themselves now at one white sun, and then at a party-colored double; to see the people on them changing customs and costumes as they change their light, and to hear their quaint discussions as they justify the new and ridicule the old.

It cost me a little effort to adjust myself to the old points of view. But I had a Mentor so loving and so patient, whose range—oh! it is infinitely before mine; and he knew how well I loved Earth, and if need had been, he would have spent and been spent till he had adjusted me to the dear old point of vision. No need of large effort, though. There it was, just as he told me. I was in the old plane of the old ecliptic. And again I saw my dear old Orion, and the Dipper, and the Pleiades, and Corona, and all the rest of them, just as if I had never seen other figures made from just the same stars when I had other points of view.

But what I am to tell you of is but one thing.

This guardian of mine and I—not bothered by time —were watching the little systems as the dear little worlds flew round so regularly and so prettily. Well, it was as in old days I have taken a little water on the end of a needle, and have placed it in the field of my compound microscope. I suppose, as I said, that just then there were several thousand solar systems in my ken at once—only the words " then," " there," and " once" have but a modified meaning when one is in these relations. I had only to choose the " epoch" which I would see. And of one world and another I had vision equally distinct—nay, of the blush on a girl's cheek in the planet Neptune, when she sat alone in her bower, I had as distinct vision as of the rush of a comet which cut through a dozen systems, and loitered to flirt with a dozen suns.

In the experience which I describe, I had my choice of epochs as of places. I think scholars or men of scholarly tastes will not wonder when I say that in looking at our dear old Earth, after amusing myself for an instant with the history of northern America for ten or twenty thousand of its years, I turned to that queer little land, that neck between Asia and Africa, and that mysterious corner of Syria which is north of it. Holy Land, men call it, and no wonder. And I think, also, that nobody will be surprised that I chose to take that instant of time when a great caravan of traders was crossing the isthmus—they were already well on the Egyptian side—who had with them a handsome young fellow whom they had bought just above, a day or two before, and were carrying down south to the slave-market at On, in Egypt.

This handsome youngster was Jussuf Ben Yacoub, or, as we say, Joseph, son of Jacob. He was handsome in the very noblest type of Hebrew beauty. He seemed eighteen or nineteen years old; I am not well enough read to know if he were. The time was early morning. I remember even the freshness of the morning atmosphere, and that exquisite pearliness of the sky. I saw every detail, and my heart was in my mouth as I looked on. It had been a hot night, and the sides of the tents were clewed up. The handsome fellow lay, his wrists tied together by a cord of camel's hair which bound him to the arm of a great Arab, who looked as I remember Black Hawk of the Sacs and Foxes. Joseph sat up, on the ground, with his hands so close to the other that the cord did not move with his motion. Then, with a queer trick, which I did not follow, and a wrench which must have been agony to him, he twisted and changed the form of the knot in the rope. Then, by a dexterous grip between his front teeth, he loosened the hold of the knot. He bit again, again, and again. Hurrah! It is loose, and the boy is free from that snoring hulk by his side. An instant more, and he is out from the tent; he threads his way daintily down the avenue between the tent ropes; he has come to the wady that stretches dry along the west flank of the encampment: five hundred yards more will take him to the other side of the Cheril-el-bar (the wall of rock which runs down toward the west from the mountains), and he will be free. At this moment two nasty little dogs from the outlying tent of the caravan—what is known among the Arabs as the tent of the warden of the route—sprang after him, snarling and yelling.

The brave boy turned, and, as if he had David's own blood in his veins, and with the precision of David's eye, he threw a heavy stone back on the headmost cur so skilfully that it struck his spine, and silenced him forever, as a bullet might have done. The other cur, frightened, stood still and barked worse than ever.

I could not bear it. I had only to crush that yelping cur, and the boy Joseph would be free, and in eight-and-forty hours would be in his father's arms. His brothers would be saved from remorse, and the world—

And the world—?

I stretched out my finger unseen over the dog, when my Guardian, who watched all this as carefully as I did, said: "No. They are all conscious and all free. They are His children just as we are. You and I must not interfere unless we know what we are doing. Come here, and I can show you."

He turned me quite round into the region which the astronomers call the starless region, and there showed me another series—oh! an immense and utterly unaccountable series—of systems, which at the moment seemed just like what we had been watching.

"But they are not the same," said my Guardian, hastily. "You will see they are not the same. Indeed, I do not know myself what these are for," he said, "unless— I think sometimes they are for you and me to learn from. He is so kind. And I never asked. I do not know."

All this time he was looking round among the systems for something, and at last he found it. He pointed out, and I saw, a system just like our dear old system, and a world just like our dear old world. The same ear-shaped South America, the same leg-of-mutton-shaped Africa, the same fiddle-shaped Mediterranean Sea, the same boot for Italy, and the same football for Sicily. They were all there. "Now," he said, "here you may try experiments. This is quite a fresh one ; no one has touched it. Only these here are not His children—these are only creatures, you know. These are not conscious, though they seem so. You will not hurt them, whatever you do : nay, they are not free. Try your dead dog here, and see what will happen."

Sure enough, there was the gray of the beautiful morning ; there was the old hulk of an Arab snoring in his tent ; there was the handsome boy in the dry valley, or wady ; there was the dead dog—all just as it happened—and there was the other dog snarling and yelping. I just brushed him down, as I have often wiped a green louse off a rose-bush ; all was silent again, and the boy Joseph turned and ran. The old hulk of an Arab never waked. The master of the caravan did not so much as turn in his bed. The boy passed the corner of the Cheril-el-bar carefully, just looked behind to be sure he was not followed, and then, with the speed of an antelope, ran, and ran, and ran. He need not have run. It was two hours before any one moved in the Midianite camp. Then there was a little alarm. The dead dogs were found, and there was a general ejaculation, which showed that the

Midianites of those days were as great fatalists as the Arabs of this. But nobody thought of stopping a minute for one slave more or less. The lazy snorer who had let him go was well lashed for his laziness. And the caravan moved on.

And Joseph? After an hour's running, he came to water, and bathed. Now he dared open his bag and eat a bit of black bread. He kept his eyes all round him; he ran no more, but walked, with that firm, assured step of a frontiersman or skilful hunter. That night he slept between two rocks under a terebinth tree, where even a hawk would not have seen him. The next day he treaded the paths along the hill-side, as if he had the eyes of a lynx and the feet of a goat. Toward night he approached a camp, evidently of a sheik of distinction. None of the squalidness here of those trading wanderers, the Midianite children of the desert! Everything here showed Eastern luxury, even, and a certain permanency. But one could hear lamentation, and on drawing near one could see whence it came. A long procession of women were beating their arms, striking the most mournful chords, and singing —or, if you please, screaming—in strains of the most heart-rending agony. Leah and Bilhah and Zilpah led the train three times around old Jacob's tent. There, as before, the curtains were drawn aside, and I could see the old man crouched upon the ground, and the splendid cloak or shawl, where even great black stains of blood did not hide the gorgeousness of the party-colored knitting, hung before him on the tent-pole, as if he could not bear to have it put away.

Joseph sprang lightly into the tent. "My father, I am here!"

Oh, what a scream of delight! what ejaculations!

what praise to God ! What questions and what answers ! The weird procession of women heard the cry, and Leah, Zilpah, and Bilhah came rushing into the greeting. A moment more, and Judah from his tent, and Reuben from his, headed the line of the false brethren. Joseph turned and clasped Judah's hand. I heard him whisper: "Not a word. The old man knows nothing. Nor need he."

The old man sent out and killed a fatted calf. They ate and drank, and were merry; and for once I felt as if I had not lived in vain.

And this feeling lasted—yes, for some years of their life. True, as I said, they were years which passed in no time. I looked on, and enjoyed them with just that luxury with which you linger over the charming last page of a novel, where everything is spring, and sunshine, and honey, and happiness. And there was the comfortable feeling that this was my work. How clever in me to have mashed that dog ! And he was an ugly brute, too ! Nobody could have loved him. Yes; though all this passed in no time, still, I had one good comfortable thrill of self-satisfaction ; but then things began to darken, and one began to wonder.

Jacob was growing very old. I could see that, from the way he kept in the tents while the others went about their affairs. And then, summer after summer I saw the wheat blight, and a sort of blast come over the olives; there seemed to be a kind of murrain among the cattle, and no end of trouble among the sheep and goats. I could see the anxious looks of the twelve brothers, and their talk was gloomy enough, too. Great herds of camels dying down to one or two mangy good-for-nothing skeletons ; shepherds coming back from the lake country driving three or four wretched sheep, and reporting that these were all that were left from three or four thousand! Things began to grow doubtful, even in the home camp. The women were crying, and the brothers at last held a great council of the head shepherds, and camel-drivers, and masters of horse, to know what should be done for forage for the beasts, and even for food at home.

I had succeeded so well with the dog that I was tempted to cry out, in my best Chaldee: "Egypt! why don't you go down to Egypt? There is plenty of corn there." But first I looked at Egypt, and found things were worse there than they were around Jacob's tents. The inundation had failed there for year after year. They had tried some wretched irrigation, but it was like feeding the hordes of Egypt on pepper-grass and radishes to rely on these little watered gardens. "But the granaries," I said—"where are the granaries?" Granaries? There were no granaries. That was but a dull set who were in the Egyptian government then. They had had good crops year in and year out, for a great many years, too. But they had run for luck, as I have known other nations to do. Why, I could see where they had fairly burned the corn of one year to make room for the fresher harvest of the next. There had been no Jussuf Ben Yacoub in the ministry to direct the storing of the harvest in those years of plenty. The man they had at the head was a dreamy dilettante, who was engaged in restoring some old carvings of some two hundred and fifty years before.

And, in short, the fellaheen and the people of higher caste in Egypt were all starving to death. That was, as I began to think, a little uncomfortably, what I had brought about when I put my finger on that ugly, howling yellow dog of the sleepy Midianite sentinel.

Well, it is a long story, and not a pleasant one; though, as I have said, as I and my companion watched it, it all went by in no time—I might even say in less than no time. All the glory and comfort of the encampments of Jacob's sons vanished. All became a mere hand-to-hand fight with famine. Instead of a set of cheerful, rich, prosperous chiefs of the pasture country, with thousands of retainers, and no end of camels, horses, cattle and sheep, here were a few gaunt, half-starved wanderers, living on such game as they could kill in a lucky hunt, or sometimes reduced to locusts, or to the honey from the trees. What grieved me more was to see the good fellows snapped up, one after another, by the beastly garrisons of the Canaanite cities.

Heaven knows where these devils came from, or how they roughed it through the famine. But here they were, in their fortresses, living, as I say, like devils, with the origins of customs so beastly that I will not stain this paper with them, and yet with a sort of craft such as we still call by the name of devilish, so that I do not wonder that they have been called Devil-worshippers, in all the literature of which I know anything. Here they were, and here they got head. I remember how disgusted I was when I saw them go down in ships into the Nile country, and clean out, root and branch, the Egyptians who were left after the famine—just as I have seen a swarm of rose-bugs settle on a rose garden and clean it out in an hour or two. There was the end of Egypt. Then I watched, with an interest not cheerful now, Dido's colony as she sailed with an immense crew of these Moloch-worshipping

Canaanites, and their beastly rites and customs, and planted Carthage. It was interesting to see poor Æneas dodging about on the Mediterranean, while Dido and her set were faring so well—or well they thought it—on the African shore.

I will own I was rather anxious now. Not but what there was something—and a great gaudy city it was—on the slopes of Mount Moriah and Zion. But it made me sick to see its worship, and I stopped my ears with my fingers rather than hear the songs. O God! the yells of those poor little children as they burned them to death in Hinnom, a hundred at a time, their own mothers dancing and howling by the fires! I cannot speak of it to this day. I dared not look there long. But it was no better anywhere else. I tried Greece; but I could make nothing of Greece. When I looked for the arrival of Danaus with his Egyptian arts and learning—Toonh, I think they called him in Egypt—why, there was no Toonh and no Egyptian arts, because these Canaanite brutes had cleared out Egypt. The Pelasgians were in Greece, and in Greece they stayed. They built great walls—I did not see for what—but they lived in cabins at which a respectable Apache would turn up his nose; and century after century they built the same huts, and lived in them. "As for manners, they had none, and their customs were very filthy." When it came time for Cadmus, there was no chance for Cadmus. Perhaps he came, perhaps he did not. All I know is that the Molochite invasion of Egypt had swept all alphabet and letters out of being, and that, if Cadmus came, he was rather more low-lived than the Pelasgians among whom he landed. Really all Greece was such a mess that I hated to follow along its crass stupidity, and the savage raids which the inhabitants of one valley made upon another. This was what I had done for them when I mashed that little yellow dog so easily.

Æneas and his set seemed to prosper better at first. I could see his ships, with the green leaves still growing on the top-masts, hurry out from the port of Dido. I saw poor Palinurus tumble over. Yes, indeed, queer enough it was to have the old half-forgotten lines of Dryden—whom I know a great deal better than Virgil, more shame to me—come back as poor Nisus plead for his friend, as poor Camilla bled to death, and as Turnus did his best for nothing. Yes, I watched Romulus and the rest of them, just as it was in Harry and Lucy's little inch-square history. I took great comfort in Brutus; I shut my eyes when the noble lady Lucretia stabbed herself; and the quick-moving stereoscope—for I really began to feel that it was one—became more and more fascinating, till we got to the Second Punic War.

Then it seemed to me as if that cursed yellow dog came to the front again. Not that I saw him, of course. Not him! His bones and skin had been gnawed by jackals a thousand years before. But the evil that dogs do lives after them; and when I saw the anxiety on Scipio's face—they did not call him Africanus—when I looked in on little private conferences of manly Roman gentlemen, and heard them count up their waning resources, and match them against the overwhelming force of Carthage, I tell you I felt badly. You see, Carthage was simply an outpost of all that Molochite crew of the East. In the history I am used to, the Levant of that time was divided between Egypt and Greece, and what there was left of Alexander's empire. But in this yellow-dog system, for which I was responsible, it was all one brutal race of Molochism, except that Pelasgian business I told you of in Greece, which was no more to be counted in the balance of power than the Digger Indians are counted in the balance to-day. This was what made poor Scipio and the rest of them so downhearted. And well it might. I, who saw the whole, as you may say, together, only, as I have explained, it did not mix itself up—I could see Hannibal with his following of all the Mediterranean powers except Italy, come down on the Romans and crush them as easily as I crushed the cur. No, not as easily as that, for they fought like fury. Men fought and women fought, boys and girls fought. They dashed into the harbor of Carthage once with fire-ships, and burned the fleet. They sent a squadron even into the port of Sidon, and burned half the city. But it was no good : army after army was beaten ; fleet after fleet was sunk by the great Carthaginian triremes. Ah me ! I remember one had the cordage of the admiral's ship made from the hair of the Roman matrons. But it was all one. If it had been Manilla hemp or wire rope, the ship would not have stood when that brutal Sidonian admiral rammed at her with his hundred oarsmen. That battle was the end of Rome. The brutes burned it first. They tumbled down the very walls of the temples. What they could plough, they ploughed. The boys and girls who were not big enough to fight they dragged into slavery, and that was the end. All the rest were dead on the field of battle, or were sunk in the sea.

And so Molochism reigned century after century. Just that, one century after another century : two centuries in all. What a reign it was ! Lust, brutality, terror, cruelty, carnage, famine, agony, horror. If

I do not say death, it is because death was a blessing in contrast to such lives. For now that there was nobody to fight who had an idea above the earth and dead things, these swords that were so sharp had to turn against each other. No Israel to crush, no Egypt, no Iran, no Greece, no Rome, Moloch and Canaan turned on themselves, and fought Canaan and Moloch. Do not ask me to tell the story! Where beast meets beast, there is no story to tell worth your hearing or my telling. Brute rage gives you nothing to describe. They poisoned, they starved, they burned; they scourged and flayed and crucified; they invented forms of horror for which our imagination, thank God, has no picture, and our languages no name. And all this time lust, and every form of pestilence and disease which depends on lust, raged as fire rages when it has broken bounds. It was seldom and more seldom that children were born; nay, when they were born, they seemed only half alive. And those who grew to manhood and womanhood—only it is desecration to use those names—transmitted such untamed beastliness to those who came after!

One hundred years, as I said. Fewer and fewer of these wretches were left in the world. I could see fields grow up to jungles and to forests. A fire wasted Carthage, and another swept away On, and another finished Sidon, and there was neither heart nor art to rebuild them. Then another hundred years dragged by, with worse horrors, if it were possible, and more. The stream of the world's life began to run in drops, now big drops, with a noisy gurgle; black drops, too, or bloody red. Fewer men, and still fewer women, and all mad with beastly rage. Every man's hand was against his brother, as if this were a world of Cains.

All this had come to them because they did not like to retain God in their knowledge.

No, I will not describe it. You do not ask me to. And if you asked, I would say "No." Let me come to the end.

The two centuries had gone. There are but a handful of these furies left. Then the last generation came—and for thirty years more of murder and fight it ground along. At the last, how strange it seemed to me, all that there are left, in two unequal parties, each of which had its banner still for fight, and a sort of uniform as if they were armies; but only four on one side and nine on the other met, as if the world were not wide enough for both, and met in that very Syria where I had helped Joseph, son of Jacob, to fling his arms round his father's neck again.

Nor, indeed, was it very far from that spot. It was close to the wreck and ruin of the Jebusite city which had been one of the strongholds last destroyed of one of these clans. That city was burned, but I saw that the ruins were smoking. Just outside there was an open space. I wonder if it had a weird, deadly look, or whether the horror of the day made me think so? I remember a great rock like a man's skull that peered out from the gray, dry ground. Around that rock these wretches fought, four to nine, hiding behind it, on one side or the other, on that April day, under that black sky.

One is down ! Two of the other party are kneeling on him, to take the last breath of life from him. With a yell of rage three or four of his party, dashing their shields on the heads of the two, spring upon them ; and I can see one wave his battle-axe above his head, when—

Did the metal attract the spark? A crash! a blaze which dazzled my eyes, and when I opened them the last of these human brutes all lay stark dead on the one side and on the other of the grim rock of Calvary!

Not a man or a woman, not a boy or a girl, left in that world!

"Do not be disturbed," said my Mentor. "You have done nothing."

"Nothing!" I groaned. "I have ruined a world in my rashness."

"Nothing," he repeated. "Remember what I told you: these are—what shall I say?—shadows, shadowy forms. They are not His children. They are only forms which act as if they were—that you and I may see and learn, perhaps begin to understand—only it passes knowledge."

As he spoke, I remembered that I moaned and struggled with him like a crying child. I was all overwhelmed by the sight of the mischief I had done. I would not be comforted.

"Listen to me," he said again. "You have only done, or wanted to do, what we all try for at first. You wanted to save your poor Joseph. What wonder?"

"Of course I did," sobbed I. "Could I have thought? Should you have thought?"

"No," said he, with that royal smile of his—"no, I should not have thought once—I could not have thought it once—till I too tried my experiments." And he paused.

Perhaps he was thinking what his experiments also were.

Then he began again, and the royal smile had hardly

faded away : "Let me show you. Or let me try. You wanted to save your poor Joseph—all sole alone."

"Yes," I said. "Why should I not want to?"

"Because he was not alone ; could not be alone. None of them were alone ; none of them could be alone. Why, you know yourself that not a rain-drop in that shower yonder but balances against a dust-grain on the other side of creation. How could Joseph live or die alone? How could that brute he was chained to live or die alone? None of them are alone. None of us are alone. He is not alone. Even He is in us, and we are in Him. But the way with men—and it is not so long, dear friend, since you were a man—the way with men is to try what you tried. I never yet knew a man—and how many have I known, thank God!—I never yet knew a man but he wanted to single out some one Joseph to help—as if the rest were nothing, or as if our Father had no plans."

"I shall never try that again!" sobbed I, after a long pause.

"'Never,'" said he, "is a long word. You will learn not to say 'Never.' But I'll tell you what you will do. When you get a glimpse of the life in common, when you find out what is the drift—shall I say of the game, or shall I say of the law?—in which they all and we all, He in us and we in Him, are living, then, oh, it is such fun to strike in and live for all!"

He paused a minute, and then he went on, hesitating at first, as if he feared to pain me, but resolutely afterward, as if this must be said :

"Another thing I notice in most men, though not in all, is this : they do not seem at first to understand that the Idea is the whole. Abraham had left Ur rather than have any part with those smoke-and-dust men—

Nature-worshippers, I think they call them. How was it that you did not see that Joseph was going down to Egypt with the Idea? He could take what they did not have there. And as you saw, in the other place, without it, why, your world died."

Then he turned round and left that horrid world of phantoms, to go back to our own dear real world. And this time I looked on TO-DAY. How bright it seemed, and how comforting to me to think that I had never touched the yellow dog, and that he came to his death in his own way!

I saw some things I liked, and some I disliked. It happened that I was looking at Zululand, when poor Prince Lulu's foot slipped at the saddle-flap. I saw the assegai that stabbed him. Had I been a trooper at his side, by his side I would have died too. But no, I was not at his side. And I remembered Joseph, and I said, " From what I call evil, He educes good."

But as Paul Decker and Theodora Bourn rode that evening there was no time nor light for reading anything as long as this. In their talk, they forgot time, forgot themselves, indeed, as has been said, and forgot the others. But at last Cæsar came to light up their palace for them, and people looked at watches, and moved back and forth, and soon it proved that again they were making a long stop. The conductor was in the telegraph office, and was trying to call.

"Well," said the gay Mrs. Fréchette, "we are independent of them. One of these gentlemen must tell us a story, as Mr. Decker did before dinner. Mr. Menet, it is your turn now."

" I will tell the party the story of General Crook and the dolls, which I told you just now. I will tell it first as little Lulu told it, and then I will tell how Mr. Grattan told it, and perhaps Paul will tell how the red-skins tell it."

And between them they told the story of

LULU'S DOLL DID IT.

WHAT LULU TOLD.

"My doll did it," said Lulu to the others.

As it happened, Meg and I came into the play-room at that moment, and I stopped to ask what her doll did.

"My doll saved three hundred people's lives, and I believe Lieutenant Grattan said perhaps she saved the country from war. She was not this doll. This is Gertrude. She was Patty—that's Gertrude's grandmother. When her head was broke—we were at Fort Darling then—she had honorable burial. Wendell and Tom fired a salute over her grave. Sometimes I think Gertrude looks like her," said Lulu, holding Gertrude in the right point of view. "She certainly has her grandmother's eyes."

All the others laughed at this, it was so exactly in the way in which visitors to their mothers talked about them.

"But what did she do, Lulu?" persisted Meg.

"I tell you she saved the lives of a whole camp of Indians. You see, the whole command was in camp at a place they called the Sweet-water Gulch—a real nice place it was, too. And the general was very anxious, papa said, and I know mamma was anxious too. Well, one day an orderly came running over to our tents, by the brook, you know, to ask if Miss Lulu had a doll. I was out fishing with Wendell, or I should have sent

Abigail. But mamma did not know, and she seized Patty, and sent her.

"She did not come back for three days, and then she came with a beautiful bunch of grapes, and some birds, from the general to me, and with his compliments to Miss Lulu—and the doll had been a peacemaker, and had saved all these people's lives.

"Yes; only wait, and I will tell you all about it.

"We were ordered—that is, not mamma and Wendell and Patty and I, but the command was ordered—to suppress an Apache rising. The Apaches were horrid, you know. They had never made peace since anybody could remember. Well, the general—he is a real good general, anyway, if he did break Patty's leg—he hates to kill the Indians. So he took us to Sweetwater Gulch, and he just waited and waited till his time came. Then he heard of these thirty lodges—that's three hundred people—all by themselves. But he never touched them. Then he heard of three lodges just a little way off, and he pounced on them, and did not kill one man. He brought them all in prisoners.

"They were horrid. I saw them the next day. They sat on the ground with their blankets round their heads. You see, they thought we should roast them and kill them. They would not speak to one of the interpreters. No; two whole days they would not say one word.

"Then the general himself and his aide, Mr. Grattan—he's real nice—went to the prison-camp themselves. And the general took one Indian girl in his arms, and Mr. Grattan took another, and they carried them to the head-quarters tent. How they did kick and scream! Wendell and I were going fishing, and as we rode out of camp we could hear those children screaming, as far, Meg, as your father's house. The general offered them sugar—and they had candy brought for them—but they just screamed and screamed for hours. They screamed till they were so tired that first one and then the other fell asleep. The general's wife had one, and I believe Mrs. Myers had the other. But they could not do anything with them. They would just kick and scream. Then, when they were asleep, the general sent for a doll, and mamma sent him my Patty.

"By and by the Indian child waked up—and the general had her on his sofa, with his Arab rug on her —and he sat where she could not see him; but he placed Patty where she could see her.

"And I suppose she forgot where she was, and she began playing with Patty. And then she called the other girl, and there was a white cotton stuffed rabbit for her. And the two little things began playing in the tent on the ground, and then the general gave them candy and sugar again. And this time they took it. And before long Mr. Grattan and the general and the two children were all four playing together, and were all great friends.

"By and by, down at the Indians' place—I mean where the prisoners were—they told the children's mother to come up to the head-quarters tent. And she came, and lo and behold! her two little girls were playing with the general and Mr. Grattan. Mr. Grattan was cutting out paper horses for them.

"Well, that began it all. The general came to be very friendly with these thirty prisoners. Then he trusted them to go to the others with a message. And they went, and they made it all up—I mean they made up the quarrel—and so there was not any war. And we were ordered off to Fort Darling. And there Patty had her bad fall, and broke her head. And she had a military funeral, as I told you. She had it because the general was so fond of her. And I always say Patty did it, and I say so now."

WHAT THE LIEUTENANT TOLD.

I was interested in what Lulu told, in her energetic way, and when I was in New York the next week, I asked at General Hancock's head-quarters when Lieutenant Grattan would come East. To my surprise and pleasure, I found he was at the Hoffman House. He had arrived that day, summoned to an inquiry about some blankets.

I called at once to see him. After we had talked about some old friends of his and mine, I asked him if he remembered Lulu and her doll Patty. He smiled with pleasure, and said that he remembered Patty very well.

"If you know the general," said Mr. Grattan, very earnestly, "you know he hates to take a drop of Indian blood if he can help it; and though he has done such wonders in keeping the peace out there—and I suppose there is not such another campaigner in the world—he is taking care of the poor creatures all the time.

"He had had a wonderful success in Oregon. Well, I will tell you of that some other day. All of a sudden, by telegraph, we were all ordered down into the Gila country—you know where—the strip we bought from Mexico—ordered to suppress the Apaches. Everybody said this time we should have to massacre them all. I know I thought so. For the Apaches had always been at war. They did not know what a treaty was; they never had made one, that was certain. It was certain, therefore, that they never broke one.

"The general never tarries, and we were soon in the valley of the Colorado. Before long, sure enough, we had stories of the red rascals everywhere. But either they did not know we were there, or they did not care. We were not there a week before a gang of them separated from the rest, and encamped within forty miles of us. The general knew to a man who they were and where. And every man in the command wanted him to pounce on them. Instead of which, he bade me, and old Andrew, a famous scout, and some fifteen dragoons, to go and hang round, without exposing ourselves, and bring him three or four prisoners—women and children—if we could.

"Oh dear, how old Andrew hated it all! 'Ef there's anything I hate,' said he, ' it's nigger-ketching; 'n I'd as lief ketch a nigger as a red man. I hate it all. But ef the general said so, et mus' be done.'

"And done it was. We snapped up three or four families the second night, clapped them all on fast horses, and were at head-quarters before noon. And never an Apache in the big party knew it. They were all so secure that these people were left half a mile below them in the cañon.

"Then it was that the general and I tried baby-tending, much as little Lulu told you. Heavens! how that child kicked and screamed! And the general's screamed worse. But he had his wife, and I, alas! had none. But I did have a sergeant's wife, a real motherly woman, and she did her best. But both brats cried themselves to sleep. It was then that the general sent for the doll. And Miss Lulu sent her Patty, if that was the name. And certainly Patty won all the blessings of the peacemakers. I shall always say 'the doll did it.'"

HOW VERMILION TOLD IT.

What Vermilion told me belongs in the story, but it was more than a year after when I first saw Vermilion.

Vermilion's real name was Chie. In the Apache language Chie means "vermilion."

I had gone to Arizona to look after some mining property—or rather some Spanish land grants—which had been left to my nieces, the two Hermance girls, by the death of Mr. Stephen Cochran. Colonel McDavitt, who knows all about mines, had agreed to go with me, and so we had come to Prescott together. I had informed myself as well as I could about the titles to the girls' lands, and as to the geography, where they were, or at least where they ought to be; and we were about to start, with one or two young men who had joined us for the adventure, when, of a sudden, Colonel McDavitt was recalled to Bangor. There came a telegram to say that his oldest boy had a violent attack of diphtheria, and it was thought he would not live.

This changed all my plans. The colonel and his nephew went to the East. A young chemist or assayer whom I had relied on did not care to go so far among savages alone, and I found that I was to be the whole of the party—poor I, who had no experience in wildernesses or in campaigning.

So I went to Governor Fremont, and I told him my story.

It proved that things were not so bad as I feared. The governor gave me an introduction to the United States officer who commanded our force in Arizona, and said he would know who was going toward the Chiquito country, if anybody was, and whether there were any chance of escort.

And so it proved that Colonel McDavitt's recall helped me to a very pleasant experience. It was that which introduced me to Vermilion.

For the colonel said at once, when I told my sad tale, that it was all right, that he had only the day before given Vermilion a furlough that he might spend two or three weeks with his friends, and he sent an orderly for Vermilion, to see if he could not go my way.

In a very few minutes Vermilion appeared himself. From the first I was pleased with him, nor had I ever to change my opinion. He was fully six feet high, well-proportioned, with large dark eyes, hair straight and perfectly black, and long, so as to cover the collar of his jacket.

To my surprise, there was no paint upon Vermilion. He wore the blue flannel fatigue jacket of the American army, with stripes of gilt braid, not usual on a fatigue jacket, which showed he was a sergeant.

I found that he was a regularly enlisted man in a corps of guides or scouts. He had really had rank as a sergeant in one or two expeditions, and so the officers humored him by letting him wear the symbols of the rank.

"Yes," he said, in wretched English, "Vermilion go two, three, four days to the east, into the hills."

And, not to tell you of the difficulties in our agreement, it was settled that we should ride together, first to his own tribe, or sub-tribe, which he was going to visit, and then he would be my guide to the region for which I had the Spanish titles. Nothing could seem fairer than the bargain.

But the next morning, when I met him by agreement at the camp, half an hour before sunrise, I found he would not start, although everything seemed ready. "Store shut," he said—"store shut ; all store shut last night. Store open—store open—all store open by and by."

"I remonstrated vainly ; offered sugar, tobácco, and even whiskey from the government stores, which I thought would honor my demands. Nothing would do but we must wait and wait till nearly eight o'clock, and then ride back into Prescott, from which I had just come, for him to go to a particular store in McDowell Street.

I was at Vermilion's mercy ; so I had to go. And then I had to sit on my horse in McDowell Street, holding Vermilion's horse, for a long half-hour, while he made his purchases. It was nine o'clock before we started. when we might have left Prescott out of sight before six. Nor could I make him tell why we stopped there, till we came to his home.

This was on the evening of our fourth day, and very hard riding it was, too. We came to a range of hills which seemed to me very cheerless, when Vermilion dismounted, and made what he told me was a "peace smoke." Then he bade me wait and watch the smoke while he rode forward alone. In a little while he came back with another Indian, who had a child on the saddle behind him. The man was Vermilion's brother ; his name, I suppose, was Yellow Ochre, and for aught I know the boy was Ultramarine. I was introduced with great form, and we then rode seven miles more through very deep cañons, till we came to the most perfectly defended place for a village. There were clefts in the rock to enter by, and others to retreat by, but a space within—yes, as big as Boston Common—of green grass, with a pretty stream running through it, and high stone walls all around, one or two hundred feet high.

We were received with all the honors. There was shouting, and singing, and every sign of joy. I was presented to big chiefs and little chiefs, and in Spanish and in English and in Apache we made protestations of eternal love to each other. Not till these ceremonies were over would Vermilion take me to one side, where, as it proved, his own wife and his own children waited for him. It was a simple home enough. One side was made of sandstone rock twenty feet high, and the other side by a large scrub oak, the branches of which touched the rock. One or two large boughs had been cut from other oaks to thicken the shade. The ground had been scooped out to make a place for some grass which was thrown in for a bed.

Vermilion's wife was glad to see him, I am sure. She told me so afterward. But she made no signs of joy. She did bring forward with genuine motherly pride their daughter, a little girl of six years old. The child was exquisitely dressed in deer-skin perfectly white, with very bright embroidery, and with a certain elegance of savage finery which surprised me.

Vermilion lifted the child off the ground, and made no pretence of concealing his pleasure that she was so tall and well. Then he went back to his horse, unrolled the pack behind the saddle, and produced that mysterious parcel which had so excited my wonder ever since we left McDowell Street on Tuesday morning. The child's mother was eager by this time, took the knife he offered, and cut the cords of the parcel. An india-rubber cover came off first, then, to their amusement and amazement, sheets and sheets of wrapping paper, and at last, in all the glory of silk and satin and ribbon and spangle, a doll with wax head and staring blue eyes!

The little girl screamed with delight, and her screams were taken up by all the family.

Indeed, it was not three minutes before the house and we were the centre of a crowd of Indians, clamoring with curiosity, and eager to see the wonder of which the fame was spreading all through the encampment.

That doll, as Lulu afterward made me certain, must have been the twin of Patty. While I was sitting groaning in the saddle, holding the two uneasy horses in McDowell Street, Vermilion had been looking through the whole stock of the Prescott dealer, till he could match Patty's accomplishments in every particular.

On the morning after our arrival the excitement the doll had created had subsided a little, and I made Vermilion tell me the whole story. I had found before this that he spoke Spanish sufficiently well, and with little difficulty I could make out the whole.

He said that before the general came down to Sweetwater Gulch, the camp of which Lulu had told me, all his own sub-tribe of Apaches " had been to the bad place."

By this phrase he meant that they had been on a raid—had been plundering stock, sheep, and horses.

" The general is a great fighter. He knows the white man's fighting. He knows the Indian's fighting. Cochise does not know better.

"The general took Vermilion asleep—and Ponce, and Yellow Tail—and her and her and her—twenty-seven in all. Not one scalp; not one gun fired. Asleep. Took them all.

"Vermilion and Ponce and Yellow Tail sang their death-songs and waited to die. Vermilion had scalped seven white men, fourteen white women and girls. It was now Vermilion's turn. Why should he not die?

"The general did not say die. The general caught the 'Blue Swan' there, and Grattan caught the 'Little Star' there, and they carried them away. Vermilion said the white men will scalp the children first, and then they will come for Vermilion."

He stopped for five minutes—not looking at me, but looking at the ground. Then he looked up with a sunny smile, such as I had seen on his face only once before.

"When the general sent to scalp Vermilion, Vermilion found the Blue Swan playing with such another as you saw last night."

The Blue Swan was playing with Patty, Lulu's doll.

And Vermilion was fairly garrulous when he told the rest: how the general sent him and Ponce and Yellow Tail on their parole to the rest of the band; how, one by one, they persuaded the others to come in; how all that band, after much suspicion, agreed on some sort of treaty with the general; how, one by one, the general engaged all of them who were good for anything as scouts or guides. It was clear enough that they liked better to have Uncle Sam's uniform on their backs, and to be fed with his rations, than to starve on occasional "finds" of acorns, seeds, or even the chance of rabbits or quail. His wife had come up by this time, and the little girl, with Patty's twin sister in her arms. The woman said, with very pathetic earnestness, " Shi tekeh shieslinjune."

I knew nothing of the words, but Vermilion said they meant, " I the flag of peace love"; and this seemed to me so pretty that I shook hands with her, smiled, kissed the child, and then, to their wonder, made her say again, " Shi tekeh shieslinjune," and wrote down the words.

The little girl then shyly held up the doll to me, and I kissed it; and Vermilion said, with the greatest seriousness, " It was the little wax woman who did it all."

CHAPTER V.

CHRISTMAS EVE.

WITH the long-drawn evening supper in the dining-car there came on the ladies of the party the certainty that their Christmas day was not to be spent in church or in family frolic. The Corneaus' vehicle would wait long at the station at Hastings. But little hope now that the bride and bridegroom, or any chance companions of theirs, would eat at their dinner. No! the Corneaus must pick up their guests from the high-ways and by-ways, for those that were bidden would certainly not be at the table.

This time the train was standing still, not at any junction or station, but on the bleak side of the Platte River, with not a house in sight, nor, indeed, with anything in sight, so dense was the blinding snow. The reason of the failure of the telegraph was now explained. In a tempest of the day before, a long snow-shed had been whirled over—posts and telegraph had gone to the ground with it, and the wreck had lain across the track in wild confusion. A strong working party had cleared away the rubbish in a fashion. But with the early afternoon a new, heavy, hard-packing storm of snow had set in upon the unprotected road, and the heaps of ruin only made points of vantage from which and upon which drifts could gather.

In short, the train was standing still this time, because it had to stand still, and the engine-driver and conductor were accepting the inevitable.

"What I say is this," said the irrepressible Mrs. Fréchette, "if we are to spend Christmas here, it shall be a merry Christmas. I am not going to mope and mourn because for once I spend my Christmas in a palace. I have always suspected that such was my destiny. Dear Mrs. Van Sandfoord, I was dreadfully disappointed when they did not choose my husband King of Bulgaria. That seemed the last chance, you know. What I propose is this: Mr. Van Sandfoord, Mrs. Hackmatack, and—and you, Mr. Fréchette, shall be a committee, to retire now, as soon as we have done our supper. No; we will retire, and you shall stay here, and you shall agree on the programme of the Christmas festivities. Every one shall be invited—the brakemen and the porters and firemen, and cooks, and all,—all the people forward, and the conductor. There is room enough, and we will have a real jolly time, as we spend

OUR CHRISTMAS IN A PALACE."

"All right," said Hector, eager to keep up the ball. "But what are we to report, dear Mrs. Fréchette? It would help us if you told us that.

"The committee will please withdraw to the kitchen end of the car."

"Report! Mr. Van Sandfoord, you are certainly not a goose. There is only embarrassment of riches. We shall sing songs and hymns. We shall tell stories and act charades. You may preach a sermon, if you like, and I will not go to sleep. I dare say Cæsar will clear up the palace, so that you can dance a clog dance, and Mr. Menet and I can waltz together. I am not going to make your report for you. Mr. Menet, please help me across. Come here, girls, and let them have the car for their consultations."

"For one," said George Hackmatack, "I offer my contribution in advance. I have in my portfolio, if Julia has not cleared it up, a Christmas story, by Mr. Collingwood."

"A Christmas story—what luck! when our stories have all been about Thanksgiving. But who is Mr. Collingwood?"

"Mr. Collingwood—oh, he is a student in that capital college at Lansing. There boys go out in the woods winters, and make themselves of use to God and man in cutting lumber. So he knows a camp by living practice, as well as Bret Harte knows it by insight and a poet's observation. If you do not say this story of his is as tender as one of Bret Harte's stories, I shall cry. Why, I read it to one of our first critics, and all he could say was that it was studied after the story, 'How Santa Claus Came to Sandy Bar.' But I said that that was a great compliment to Bret Harte, for Mr. Collingwood studied this story in the very woods of which he tells."

All this George Hackmatack told them as the palace party gathered under Cæsar's lamps, leaving their committee behind them.

The committee came in while he was talking. It proved that they had adjusted their report to meet what he had said. Hector then stepped forward, to the very front of the passage-way, and read, in an oratorical tone, from a large sheet of paper,.

THE COMMITTEE'S REPORT.

CHAPTER VI.

THE COMMITTEE'S REPORT AND WHAT FOLLOWED.

1. Every prince and princess—that is all dwellers in the palace—shall hang up a stocking to-night outside the curtain, lest Santa Claus be disappointed.
2. Breakfast will be served at eight-thirty. All princes and princesses not present will be killed. Quail on toast, broiled chicken, fried oysters, antelope steak, and buffalo's hump.
3. Gathering in the palace at ten. The whole train invited—and the inviting party. Milton's hymn, Sears's hymn, and such other music as the choir selects to be sung by the company. Singing led by Mr. Menet, Mrs. Van Sandfoord, and Professor Wisner.

[Professor Wisner was one of the passengers forward.]

4. At eleven, the party meets again—strict punctuality—for literary exercises.

    I. Mr. Hackmatack reads Mr. Collingwood's story.
    II. Mrs. Fréchette sings an original ballad.
    III. Mr. Menet delivers an oration.
    IV. Mrs. Fréchette makes a confession.
    V. Mrs. Van Sandfoord relates the history of her life.
    VI. Mr. Fréchette reads an essay.
    VII. Mrs. Hackmatack tells how her children had the mumps.

VIII. Prayer in "Moses in Egypt," sung by the company, led by Mrs. Fréchette.
IX. The Apache's Revenge, a tableau, by Mr. Decker and Professor Wisner.
X. A historical essay on the uses of Christmas, by Mr. Hector Van Sandfoord.
XI. Intermission for dinner.

BILL OF FARE.

Buffalo hump.
Antelope steaks.
Wild turkey.
Tame turkey.
Fried oysters.
Broiled chicken.
Hog.
Hominy.
Canned peaches.
Plum pudding with burning brandy.

XII. One hour for naps and digestion.
XIII. Love story by Mr. Fréchette.
XIV. Duet from "Figaro," by Mrs. Fréchette.
XV. Bravura by Miss Bourn.
XVI. Blood-and-thunder story, by Mr. Hackmatack.
XVII. Cantata from "Fidelio," by Mrs. Fréchette.
XVIII. The Declaration of Independence, repeated from memory, by Mrs. Van Sandfoord.
XIX. A treatise on the moral law, by Mrs. Fréchette.
XX. The history of Troy, by Mrs. Fréchette.
XXI. Readings from "Romeo and Juliet," by Mrs. Fréchette.

XXII. The compact in the cabin of the Mayflower, by Mrs. Fréchette.
XXIII. The constitution of California, by Mrs. Fréchette.
XXIV. The Children in the Wood, by Mrs. Fréchette.

"Stop, stop, stop!" cried that lively lady. "You will keep us here till May-day before you have done. But I will do my part, all of you do yours, and we will have a merry Christmas.

"Dear William," she said to her husband in a stage whisper, "do go forward with my key to the baggage-car, open my small trunk, and bring me the largest pair of stockings you can find."

And so they fell to singing songs, and Christmas eve, after all, passed gayly.

Before they bade good-night, Paul Decker whispered to Mrs. Van Sandfoord:

"I am going to make you a present. Is there any harm in my giving a little picture to Miss Bourn?"

"Harm! not a bit of it; it is all a frolic, of course. I am glad I am to have one. Good-night."

"Good-night."

CHAPTER VII.

CHRISTMAS MORNING.

AND so the next morning there was great laughing and rattle as the stockings were opened.

Mrs. Fréchette took command. She was as fresh and pretty in her jaunty morning dress as if she had a party at breakfast in the *Athenée*. She was dressed early—and cried aloud : " No one is to open a stocking till all are ready, and then come all together here.

" I wish you a Merry Christmas and a Happy New Year."

And then from every curtain there echoed her joyous cry :

" Merry Christmas and Happy New Year."

Every sort of riff-raff was in the stockings—oranges, nuts, raisins, old jack-knives, little hemlock cones done up in dainty jewel-boxes, and sometimes the bona-fide presents, which had been hidden away for this morning. Paul Decker's presents to the rest were all spirited little drawings on cards. Perhaps he had some of them in his pack. Clearly enough he had drawn most of them by the baggage-master's lantern, after the party had broke up for the night before. For they were little sketches of things that had happened or had been talked of the day before. To Mrs. Van Sandfoord he gave a little picture of his great-grandfather reading Governor Trumbull's Thanksgiving Proclamation. To Miss Bourn he gave a spirited drawing of Joseph—well conceived, in a vigorous attitude—just drawing back his stone to throw it at the yelping dog.

Here he had washed in a little paint. Faces and rocks showed their colors.

And the yelping dog was yellow.

The presents made no end of fun, and the breakfast which followed was jolly beyond compare.

So was struck happily the key-note of the day.

It was fairly ten o'clock when the palace was quite full with three times the number of its regular occupants. The Christmas party had made itself up exactly as the wily proposer of it had suggested.

Professor Wisner and his associates had taken faithfully in hand the duty given them. Really he led in the singing, in that noble baritone voice which has charmed and won so many assemblies so much larger. They had taken possession of the baggage-car for practice, and, as they sang, the tears stood in the eyes of more than one of those around ; and, when there was a chance for a chorus, the company joined with a devotion and tenderness that St. Stephen's or the Vatican might envy.

Christmas began with a devout strain, harmonizing well with the key, as it should do.

One hymn and another, indeed, filled up well-nigh an hour with chatter and consultation as to times between.

At eleven Hector Van Sandfoord stood on the coal-box, and with a loud voice he said : "Ladies and gentlemen, we have only too little time for our programme. You will give your attention to Mr. Hackmatack, and he will read to you Mr. Collingwood's original Christmas tale, called

"CHRISTMAS IN COONEY CAMP."

The citizens of Cooney Camp were considerably excited. I do not wish to be understood as implying that social life at Cooney Camp was usually very stagnant. It has always been known as the liveliest camp on the river, and nobly did its citizens strive to sustain its reputation. But there was something so strange about the present excitement that I feel it my duty to chronicle it.

Cooney's was simply a lumber camp in the wild north woods of Michigan. In a little clearing on the side of a high hill a few rough log buildings were gathered. The public buildings were not known by any high-sounding names. They were simply the "Men's Shanty," the "Cook's Shanty," and the "Foreman's Shanty." These, with barns and sheds, and a few small log houses for such lumbermen as could be induced to bring their families into the woods, made up the whole of the settlement.

But if the architectural development of Cooney Camp was of an inferior quality, its society was, to use a camp phrase, "way up." The thirty lumbermen who made up its working force were, for the most part, as rough specimens of humanity as could well be found. They were proud of the fact that they could produce two fiddlers, five singers, and one gentleman who could play numberless airs on a "mouth-organ."

Heavy literary work was not, perhaps, much in their line, but if occasion required they could produce Frank, a college student, who had come into the woods in the hope of finding health and strength in the rough out-door life.

But greater than all these attractions, the point

wherein Cooney's stood far ahead of other camps, was the fact that she possessed the society of "two wimmin an' a kid." The foreman's wife kept house for her husband in the little log shanty nearest the wood, while on the other side of the clearing, opposite the "Men's" shanty, lived "Cracknosed ' Smith, with his wife and little girl.

Smith had been given his nickname from the singular appearance of his nose. This member had been broken and twisted and cracked, until it was unlike any other nose ever seen.

Cooney Camp could easily have dispensed with the society of Cracknose, but it would have been hard work to get along without the little girl. She was the pride of the camp, the brightest, dearest, little bud of humanity that ever attempted to blossom in such a rough place. She was like a delicate mountain flower growing alone among bare, bleak rocks.

I remember one day that "Cracknose" attempted to whip her. A dozen men at once informed him, in the forcible language of Cooney Camp, that if he touched her they would thrash him within an inch of his life.

It is needless to say that the whipping was postponed.

But, as we started to say, there was a strange excitement in Cooney Camp.

It was Christmas eve, and some little reflection of the happiness and good-cheer in the world outside seemed to have fallen upon the camp.

The men came in from their work in the woods in great good humor. It is wonderful how, at such a time, the true nature of a man shines out, and how little, foolish, blundering acts betray a warm heart beneath a rough exterior. Each man, as he came into camp, brought, half foolishly, some little Christmas token. It was only a bunch of hemlock branches, or a bunch of red berries, or, perhaps, some fragrant cedar boughs; but, slight as they were, the little tokens showed their appreciation of the day.

In a more civilized community it would have been considered a very simple thing for a man to pick up a bit of green at Christmas, but with these rough fellows it was different. Here was red-haired Tom, who had killed a man in the next county, coming in with a bunch of winter berries. Here was Jake, who kicked an Indian out of doors but the week before, dragging in a great mass of hemlock, and even old Bill coming in with a great tree on his back, which he proceeded to decorate with old boots and shoes, to the great delight of the boys. Every one was good-natured, and all were bent on having a good time.

Hugh, the first fiddler, put a new string in his violin, and having found its tone to be perfect, laid it carefully away in his bunk till after supper.

Mike and Fred appointed themselves a committee of arrangements, and announced that, as soon as supper was over, the floor would be cleared for a "two by four," that being the camp name for a square dance.

Supper was eaten in a great hurry, and back the men rushed to the shanty, and took their places on the floor to walk through the great "two by four."

Sing, ye muse, of a pine wood's dance! The men stand in place, with their outer clothing tossed aside, ready at the signal to throw themselves into the motion. Those who are to impersonate ladies are distinguished from the others by removing their hats. They stand as solemn as owls in the consciousness of their new dignity, and "gallivant left" and "ladies chain" with becoming modesty. The fiddler sits above them on an empty pork-barrel, with his fiddle clasped lovingly under his chin, ready to set the party in motion at the touch of his magic bow. The lantern hangs from a nail in the roof. The fire-light flashes over all, bringing out the rough walls and empty bunks in bold relief.

So the Cooney campers stood that Christmas eve, waiting for the signal, when the door opened, and in rushed old Jack—gruff, grizzled old Jack, the roughest, ugliest, and most profane man in camp.

"Shet up this yer old circus," he shouted, "an' hark what I tell ye."

The "set" broke up in a moment. Hugh dropped his fiddle and bow, and Mike, who was to "call off," stood silent, with his mouth open in the very act of ordering "s'lute pardners."

"Thar's a man in this yar camp," said Jack, "ez wants humpin'. It kinder come over me all ter onst, thet I'd go up ter Smith's, an' git his woman an' kid ter come down an' see the fun. But when I gut thar, blame me ef he warn't layin' ez drunk ez a loon, with his woman a-yellin', an' thet little kid jest a-lookin' at him with them big eyes of hern. Now blame me ef it's right. Somethin' orter be did."

Jack's story was, I regret to say, true. Poor "Cracknose," being anxious to celebrate the day in a manner becoming his birth and education, had provided himself with a large bottle of whiskey. He had partaken so frequently of his Christmas cheer, however, that he was already, as Jack expressed it, "drunk as a loon."

A howl of indignation went up from the crowd as Jack finished. It may be that the indignation of some of the boys was not unmixed with envy at Smith's good fortune in securing the wherewithal to get "drunk as a loon." There were probably very few men in camp who, had they possessed the means, would not have speedily drunk themselves into Smith's condition. They had all enough manhood, however, to despise one who would get drunk before his woman and kid, and such a little kid, too. They certainly believed with Jack that Smith deserved a "humpin'" of the most advanced kind.

What should be done about it? Unconsciously the men resolved themselves into a committee of the whole to consider the matter. It was a serious question.

"I moves," said Barney, the logical man of camp, "I moves that we sends up a '*ker*mithy.'"

"*Ker*mithy be hanged," put in Jack; "the only '*ker*mithy' yer want is a *ker*mithy to go up thar an' thump the life out of Smith, an' I app'ints myself as cheerman of said '*ker*mithy.'" Then he added quickly, "Is they any remarks? Ef not, them ez stands by it say aye!"

There was a loud chorus of "aye!" Anything in the shape of a free-fight was to be encouraged by all possible means in Cooney Camp.

Jack went on, "Them ez is agin it say 'No,' an' I'll thump their heads fer them." Not a word was said, and the motion was certainly carried. Jack's fist was too heavy to admit of much argument. Some of the voters could hardly see the practical good of "thumping the life" out of a man who was already dead drunk, but they were silent from prudential motives.

Jack "app'inted" Tom and Bill as other members of the "*ker*mithy," and the three worthies started out.

The rest of the men stood at the door of the shanty and watched them.

A bright light shone from the window of Smith's house, and through it the "kermithy" stole by the corner, and held a whispered consultation. Then Jack stepped up to the window and looked in. But what was the matter with him? Why did he not go in with the "kermithy," and proceed to "thump the life out of Smith"?

He stood looking in at the window, and presently his hard old hand stole up and took off the rough cap he wore. He stood without a covering in the cold night air. This was too much for the endurance of the waiting crowd. To be sure they had sent the "kermithy" to do their work, but if its members refused to serve, they must take the matter into their own hands. As one man, they ran as silently as possible through the snow and looked over Jack's shoulder. If any of them had any inclination to be noisy, the sight that met their eyes silenced them in a moment.

The same scene was being enacted, no doubt, in thousands of homes at that time, but nowhere under the same circumstances. The little "kid" was just going to bed, and was kneeling, as children do, before her mother to say her prayers. At the back of the room lay Cracknose in a drunken sleep. In front sat the mother, listening to the little girl, and correcting her when she forgot a word. The poor woman had been crying, and the great tears stood in her eyes, as she watched the small petitioner.

The little one went slowly through the old "Now I lay me down to sleep," and then began a prayer of her own, speaking in her baby voice so that the crowd outside could hear her: "Dod bess everybody, and pease let old Santy Caus put a dolly in my stockin'—dood-night." There was nothing more. The woman caught the child in her arms and burst out crying, while the audience outside stole silently back to the shanty.

Not a word was spoken. Jack and his "kermithy" had forgotten their mission of thumping the life out of Smith, and there was not a man in camp who would call upon them to "rise and report progress."

The childish prayer had touched a chord in the hearts of the rough lumber-men that had been long forgotten. It gave them all a new idea for their Christmas.

The dance was forgotten. Hugh silently laid his fiddle away, and the company stood waiting for Jack, the acknowledged leader, to speak.

"Who *is* this yer blame 'Santy' Claus?" said he at last with a scowl.

The boys tried to tell him. Most of them, perhaps, had seen a Christmas tree, and had watched the good old saint enter with his bells and great beard. But not one of them could explain. They were like great children.

At last, Ira, who, as the head of a large and constantly increasing family, was supposed to be posted on home matters, began:

"Wall, he's a man; an ole man, ye see—"

"Wall," put in Jack, "he wants ter bring thet blame doll-baby ter-night, or I'll lick the face offen him."

"But ye can't do it," argued Ira.

"Can't!" yelled Jack. "Who says I can't? How big is he? What will he weigh? I'll fight him ef he weighs a ton."

"But ye see," explained Ira, "he ain't no *man* at all; only a kinder—wall, a kinder *thing* ez comes around an' fills the kids' stockin's—only he don't fill 'em at all, ye see. Ye see the folks they puts the truck in themselves, an' then 'lows ter the kids thet this yer 'Santy' Claus must hev done it. The kids they kinder takes it all in, an'"—and Ira proceeded to tell all the simple story.

Old Jack listened attentively. "An' so this yer hull bizness is a derned 'give' on thet kid, is it? Blame me ef it's white ter swap lies with sech a kid ez thet. Ye jest wait till I see inter this a bit"—and out he strode to Smith's cabin.

The crowd wonderingly followed him at a respectful distance, and while he went in, they gathered again outside.

Through the window they could see that the little girl had at last gone to bed. Her small, blue stocking, patched and worn, hung from a nail by the bed, all ready for Santa Claus and the doll.

Jack came out at last, and walked straight to the shanty, the crowd following him. Without a word he pulled on his coat and fur cap.

"The woman says she ain't gut no doll-baby fer the kid, an' ez Santy Claus ain't *nuthin'*, I'm jest gonter fill thet stockin' myself. Who'll walk ter Crystal with me an' git some truck fer it?"

Every man in camp shouted: "I will."

"I don't want but one uv ye—draw lots," said Jack.

Thirty little blocks of wood were quickly prepared, and on one of them was written the word "go." These were shaken in a cap, and it was agreed that the one drawing the marked block should accompany Jack.

As a compliment to his supposed literary ability Frank was appointed to hold the hat. The men crowded around him, all anxious to get a chance to do something for the "kid."

One after another the blocks were taken out. They were all blanks. At last there were only two left and Bill and Frank to draw. Bill drew first and took out a blank. Frank was to go with Jack and act as Santa Claus. They pulled on their rough coats and hats, and started at once.

Crystal was ten miles away by the road, but by going through the forest one mile each way could be saved. Jack determined to try the nearest way, and immediately started up the hill into the forest, leaving Frank to follow as best he could.

The men stood at the shanty door, and watched them till they passed out of sight under the trees.

It was a beautiful night. The stars were all out, and the moon shone through the trees, glancing on the frost-covered branches, till they sparkled like diamonds.

A gentle breeze blew softly through the forest. The thin-leaved cedars whispered and rustled their down-growing branches. The clustering hemlocks held the wandering breeze for a moment to send it on again, freighted with a rude harmony, while the great pines spread out their long, needle-like, numberless Æolian harps to swell the grand symphony of nature.

Jack strode on ahead, like his namesake of old who wore the seven-leagued boots.

How he did walk! Logs, stumps, brush were as nothing to him. He plunged and pushed and dodged his way along, ever keeping straight ahead for Crystal. Frank could hardly keep him in sight.

Perhaps it was due to this fact, or that this was his

first experience as Santa Claus, that Frank began to doubt the wisdom of the journey. He began to fear that they had come on a very ridiculous errand. Why should they walk twenty miles through the frozen snow simply to procure a "doll-baby" for that little girl? The idea was absurd! How much more comfortable they would be in camp by the fire!

Jack seemed to have been thinking in much the same way, for he waited on a log for Frank to overtake him. Then he began: "Wot blamed fools we be—ain't we? Here we be drivin' off here hell-bent fer 'lection, jest fer a kid. It beats all." Then he added apologetically, "Ye see some blamed fool hez ben swappin' lies with thet kid, an' she takes it all in! The lie's told, an', hang me, ef I don't stand by it. She'll find out soon nuff thet this yer Santy Claus is a derned whelp, an' I'm in for makin' her think he's all straight ez long ez I kin."

After this oration Jack started again, while Frank struggled after him as best he could.

Rough old Jack! He had hardly been known to do a good deed before; what could have sent him on such a tramp? Of what was he thinking, as he struggled through the woods on that cheerless journey to Crystal? Perhaps the words of the little "kid" came to him even then, "Dod bess everybody." Perhaps the little voice had wakened in his tough old heart some memory that had lain slumbering for years.

At any rate, in his rough way, he had spoken the right idea. What was the long, cold walk, after all, to the thought that by taking it they kept alive the little one's faith in the old story of Christmas, and staved off, for a while at least, the knowledge of the deceit and heartlessness of the world?

Presently Jack stopped again. "This yer blamed Santy Claus in this yer play comes down the chimbly, don't he?"

Frank stated that this was his favorite way of entrance.

"Wall, thar ain't no chimbly ter thet shanty, nuthin' but a stove-pipe. I'll 'low thet I'll jab a hole through the ruff with my axe, so we can kerry out the hull blamed play."

On they pressed, mile after mile, till, at last, after climbing an unusually steep hill, they looked down upon a clearing, in which stood, perhaps, a half dozen small houses clustered around a saw-mill. "Here we be," said Jack—"here's Crystal."

There was something weird and romantic in the sight as they looked down upon the little hamlet.

The village was built in a small clearing, which looked to the two representatives of Santa Claus on the hill as if some huge giant in his rage had pulled out a great handful of the forest. The snow lay deep on the ground, and great blackened stumps stood all about the clearing, like sentinels watching while the village slept. The moonbeams played over all, bringing out each ghostly corner and hole, while the tall smoke-stack of the saw-mill rose in the midst like a watch-tower.

But Jack and Frank had no time for such romantic thoughts as these. They hurried down the one street of the village, until Jack stopped before a small log-house, and began a vigorous kicking upon its door. On a shingle over this door Frank read in black, straggling letters, " Poste Offis "—" Goods to Traide."

Jack warmed his toes on the door, till above it a small window opened, and a man's head appeared.

"Open up, yer old brute," roared Jack. The head had evidently just pulled itself out of bed, and seemed to belong to a very profane man ; for, in a loud voice, it forcibly informed the citizens of Crystal that it hadn't gut no whiskey ner no "terbacky."

This announcement of the lack of these two staples had but little effect on Jack. He shouted back : "We wanter git some Christmas truck, so open up yer door, or I'll kick it down," and he proceeded to bestow upon it a series of kicks that would soon have caved it in, had not the owner profanely agreed to "open up."

In a short time he appeared at the door, and grumbled as he bade them enter.

Jack and Frank passed into the little store. But now, for the first time since the start, Jack hung back. He could walk or fight or swear for the "kid," but selecting presents for her stocking was more than he could do.

He pushed Frank ahead, saying : "You know something about these things, jest pick out yer truck, an', mind ye, I'll pay fer it."

The stock of goods at the "Crystal Emporium" was not very extensive. One could find plenty of flour or sugar or pork, but the purely holiday goods were almost gone.

After a careful search, however, Frank found a few nuts, an old Jew's-harp, a jumping-jack with only one leg which could possibly be induced to jump, a tin whistle with a most melancholy sound, and, as luck would have it, a large orange. There were also a few ounces of cheap candy, which Frank took with many misgivings. He feared its effect on the stomach of the little stocking-hanger. This was all.

Jack was detemined to find a doll. "The kid wants a doll-baby, an' hang me ef she don't hev it ef I have to walk fifty miles fer it."

The merchant prince of Crystal, evidently anxious to return to bed as quickly as possible, suggested that his woman could "kinder slip a sorter dress like onter the jumpin'-jack so it could pass fer a doll-baby."

This started Jack's ire at once. "Ye don't ring no jumpin'-jack with one sound leg off onter me. I tell ye I want a doll-baby with two sound legs an' plenty of fixin's."

Just at this point the merchant's wife came downstairs to try and settle the dispute. She was such a motherly-looking person that Frank took heart and told her the whole story of the little girl's prayer, and her want of a dolly.

The woman was probably a very practical person. She could hardly have been otherwise, living as she did in such a place. But in every woman's heart there lies a spot that the smallest, weakest little child can touch to life.

She thought for a moment, and then pulled back an old blanket which hung at one end of the room, and pointed to a rough bed in which lay two children asleep. Over their heads hung two little stockings, crowded full of trinkets for them to see in the morning.

Jack stood and looked in wonder. All he could say was, "Santy Claus done it!"

The good woman took a small package from one of the stockings, and handed it to the astonished Jack, saying: "Here is a doll for you. It is the best we can do."

There may have been a tear in her eye as she thought of the little girl far away in the woods, but this fact did not prevent her genial husband from remarking, incidentally, that the doll was "wuth jest about two shillin's."

Jack and Frank gathered their treasures and started back. They hurried up the steep hill into the forest, meaning to follow their track back to camp.

They had hardly gone a mile before Jack turned to Frank and said, "It's gonter cloud up—we must make fer the road an' foller it inter camp." Quickly they turned to the right, and struck out through the woods for camp.

But not quite quick enough. Great black clouds came rushing over the sky, and, one by one, the stars were hid from sight. Under the trees the darkness was complete.

Jack and Frank wandered on, as best they could, apparently going deeper and deeper into the forest, and yet unable to correct their way.

Suddenly Jack fell down over a log and lay with a groan. He was up soon, however. His hand was hurt somewhat, and his leg caught under a limb. As he pulled his leg away from its fastening, Frank asked him how his hand felt. "Dern the hand," he growled; "wait till I see ef thet doll-baby is broke."

The toy was uninjured, and when this had been ascertained, on they started once more.

At last Jack stopped. "This thing hez gut ter be broke. We kin live out here well 'nuff till mornin', but the p'int is ter git back ter fill thet stockin'. Wait till I build a fire. P'raps the boys will see it."

Jack soon found a dry cedar, with which he quickly built a fire at the foot of a huge pine. The flames went roaring up into the air, and by their light the two Christmas commissioners saw the long-desired road but a few rods away. They had been travelling by the side of it in the wrong direction.

They had still eight miles to go, and tired as they were, it was nearly three o'clock before they came in sight of camp.

They knew that the boys would be waiting for them at the shanty, but Jack had become suddenly independent. "Say, what's the use fer the hull crowd ter go inter this thing? Why not I an' you jest do this work, an' hev it *did?*"

Jack's word in such a case was surely law, and so the two men crept by the shanty to the little house, each one a very guilty Santa Claus, quite unlike his jovial, happy self.

There was no jingle of bells or pulling in of reindeer, but just two men in rough clothing, half ashamed of their errand, creeping like convicts through the cold. They pushed open the door of the rude cabin, and entered as silently as possible. The lamp was turned low, and the fire burned dimly.

Smith lay as before. His wife had, perhaps, surmised Jack's errand, and tried to sit up for him, but, worn out by watching, she was sleeping in her chair by the table.

The little girl lay asleep with her pretty hair straggling down over the pillow. Frank filled the stove with wood, while Jack hastily thrust the few simple presents into the stocking. Though he did not know it, he looked like a veritable Santa Claus with his grizzled beard and rough fur cap.

The stocking was full, and yet Jack lingered. The orange could not be induced to enter the stocking, so he laid it on the pillow by the side of the little sleeper. Perhaps the child-face on the pillow was too much for him, for, as if moved by a sudden impulse, he bent over and kissed the tiny rosebud of a mouth.

The little one woke for a moment, and asked in her baby-voice, "Is you Santy Caus?"

"No! be hanged ef I be," said Jack, and then, remembering where he was, he blushed, as nearly as he could, through his red face.

The two impersonators of Santa Claus stole silently from the cabin. As they went, Jack growled in his old threatening way, "If ye tell the boys of thet, I'll lick ye till ye can't see."

Thus was the one stocking filled in Cooney Camp. Santa Claus *did* find his way over the rough winding road, and, guided by a strange, tender, and beautiful power, he stopped at the poor cabin on the hill. What though he *did* come without his sleigh or his bells! What though the journey left him weary, cold, and lame! He came and did his work and went his way with a lighter and purer heart than he had known for years.

The Christmas sun came dancing over the tops of the trees before many of the inhabitants of Cooney Camp were stirring.

The cook had been up for an hour, working away in his shanty at the Christmas breakfast. He had not much material with which to work, but, by taking extra care with his fried pork, and boiling the potatoes without their skins, he hoped to be able to win the applause of the crowd. He had also a surprise in the shape of several dried-apple pies, with which he thought to achieve a grand triumph.

But the rest of the Cooney Campers were for the most part still in their bunks. Sunday was always a day of rest. It was the great day for card-playing and dancing, and when Christmas came on the same day, they surely could not think of getting up as early as usual. So they lay in their bunks and waited till the horn blew, when they sprang to the floor and hastily prepared for breakfast.

Not a word was said about the events of the previous night. There seemed to be a tacit agreement that the subject should not be mentioned, yet it was noticed after breakfast that there was a general desire to see how Smith was "gittin' over his drunk."

In delegations of two and three the lumbermen visited his cabin, and it is safe to say that on that Christmas he received more visitors than on any previous celebration of the holiday.

The visitors came back with wonderful stories of the liberality of Santa Claus. It seemed to be understood that they should ignore entirely their knowledge of the journey to Crystal, and seek to carry out the less probable but more romantic theory of Santa Claus and his deer and bells.

"I'll be hanged," said Tom thoughtfully, "ef this yer Santy Claus ain't done a big thing. Talk about yer play truck—I tell ye thet kid hez gut some ez lays over the largest. Leavin' out thet doll-baby, thar's a figger of a man with a string hangin' down betwixt his legs, an' when ye yank the string, I'm derned ef the off leg won't kick ter beat all."

The unexpected visit of the good old saint had started all the latent æstheticism which had thus far lain dormant in Cooney Camp. There was a general overhauling of old clothes, in the hope of finding a clean shirt or a paper collar. Several of the men even expressed a desire to shave; and at last, Barney, after carefully sharpening his knife on the grindstone, opened an impromptu barber's shop in one corner of the shanty.

Even old Jack caught the infection. He pulled out from somewhere in his bunk a soiled paper collar, which he proceeded to pin, with great gravity, to his flannel shirt. This, with a little sprig of pine in the button-hole of his vest, made up the extras of his Christmas costume. He made a desperate effort to bring his mop of hair into some sort of shape, but gave it up after a violent struggle.

After making all his preparations, he lounged about the shanty, evidently ill at ease. It may have been the paper collar or the fear of ridicule from the boys that troubled him. He evidently wished to go over to Smith's, and yet could hardly summon up courage enough to start.

As a fighter Jack was supreme. In woodcraft or in all the social qualities which became lumbermen, he had no superior; but at making Christmas calls, or at framing excuses for a visit, the smallest boy could beat him easily. He blundered about to find some pretence for going over to see what the little girl thought of Santa Claus.

The other boys had been anxious "to see how Smith was gittin' over his drunk," but Jack took a more probable reason for going. He 'lowed at last that he'd go over an' see ef Smith hed drinked up all his whiskey. He felt kinder picked, an' 'lowed he could emp't the bottle dern soon. It was a good sight better fer a man ter drink it ez hed head enough ter keep right side up.

Transparent as this excuse was, it was enough for the boys. They said nothing, and Jack, fortifying himself with an immense piece of tobacco, strolled carelessly over to Smith's house. He stopped long enough at the door to throw a long stream of tobacco juice over the white snow, and then pushed it open and went in.

Quite a number of the boys were there already, and the little girl was holding a regular levee in one corner. She was displaying her treasures in great glee.

Barney sat with the doll carefully held between two of his great fingers. Bill had the poor jumping-jack, pulling the string, and making the one sound leg belabor the air most violently.

Hugh, the musician of the camp, was extracting a very melancholy tune from the Jew's-harp, while Mike blew a doleful blast on the tin whistle. Mrs. Smith, busy over the stove, looked at the jolly crowd, and smiled for the first time in many days. Even " Cracknose" himself, blear-eyed and weak-kneed and lightheaded from his Christmas celebration, seemed to catch something of the fun and good-will of the moment.

Jack nodded gruffly to the company, and taking a stick of wood from the pile behind the stove, made himself an impromptu seat against the wall. He forgot his supposed errand in regard to the whiskey, but sat and watched the group around the happy little " kid" in the corner.

It may be because Jack was the leader of the camp, and hence deserved more attention, or it may be that something told the little maid that he was a relative of Santa Claus. At any rate, she gathered her treasures in her apron, and came and stood by his knee to show them.

If one of the men had dared to insinuate that in all Jack's nature there was the least touch of softness or gentleness, he would have been knocked down at once. The little face of the child, however, looking into his, saw something of the kind. She climbed fearlessly upon his knee, and spread out her presents for him to see.

Jack was in a most awkward position. It was strange that he did not make her get down. But there he sat, handling the doll and the jumping-jack, and even attempting a tune on the Jew's-harp.

The little girl was loud in her praise of Santa Claus. She had seen him, too. She was awake, she said, while he was filling the stocking, and had a good chance to see him. He looked, she thought, very much like Jack himself.

This was, perhaps, the greatest compliment that the little one could give, but it almost made Jack blush for shame to think he was so near being discovered.

He made haste to throw the "kid" off the track by describing an imaginary meeting with Santa Claus. The others listened with grave faces, nodding their heads encouragingly at each point.

"Ye see," said Jack, "I run onter this yer Santy Claus myself last night. I cum out of the shanty about twelve o'clock, like enuff, an' I seen a man climbin' on the ruff of yer house. I 'lowed it might be Santy, so I jest slipped behind a stump, and watched him. Sure 'nuff it were Santy. He had a big kinder bag on his back, chuck full of all kinds of truck. He had on a fur hat, and a kinder shirt made out of skin, an' a pair uv light 'pickydilly' pants, an' a pair of rubber boots. He clumb along the ridge-pole, an' kinder stopped by the stove-pipe jest like he wuz comin' down. He histed up one foot an' stuck it inter the pipe, but thar in stuck. It wouldn't go down, an' Santy, he jest yanked it out, an' jumped up an' down, he wuz ser mad. Then he come down frum the ruff, an' kinder pushed agin the door an' went in. I 'low he must hev filled the stockin' then. Then he come out an' started off down the road playin' a tune on jest sech a Jew's-harp ez this one here. I 'low it must hev ben the mate to it."

The little girl listened in open-mouthed wonder to Jack's story, but Smith amazed the crowd by beginning to cross-question the narrator.

" Ye sed he hed on a fur cap, didn't ye ?"

" Wall, yes, I 'low I sed so !"

" Did he hev a big nose, an' kinder gray beard, an' red hair, an' a pair of kinder brown pickydillies ?"

" Wall, p'raps he did, an' then agin p'raps he didn't. What is it ter ye *ef* he did or *ef* he didn't ; he didn't hev no call ter put truck in your stockin', did he ?" growled out Jack, for he felt that he was being pushed into a corner.

Smith meekly admitted that " in course" it warn't nothin' ter him, but he kinder hed an idee thet Santy Claus must hev looked jest like unto a man ez he knowed onct. The best feller ter drink he ever see. He had seen him with his own eyes *set* by a bar, an' drink frum a dozen ter twenty glasses, an' never git " set up." It beat all how that man could drink, and Smith sighed as he thought of the moral effect he might produce on the community if *he* could only drink an unlimited quantity of whiskey without " getting set up."

This explanation started all the bile in Jack's nature. To think of associating Santa Claus with a champion drinker was too much, even for him. Not that he was a special advocate of temperance. In fact, if one had wished to give him a most particular compliment, he had only to speak of him as Smith spoke of his friend. But to his mind, Santa Claus was a different sort of personage. Besides, there was the danger of his mixing up his story, if the subject was continued.

He turned on poor Smith with his battery of sarcasm. "Shet up, you whelp," he roared. "Hang me, ef you ain't mean 'nuff ter steal corn from afore a blind sow."

There was something so terrible in this statement, that Smith cowered before it.

But Jack was not satisfied. "Jest roust out thet thar bottle o' yourn, an' I'll larn ye how ter drink without gittin' set up."

Smith dared not refuse, but at once produced his bottle of Christmas beverage from its hiding-place in an old boot in the corner. No doubt he expected to see Jack empty it down his own throat, yet his mind may have been buoyed up by the thought that he might possibly get some little insight into the secret of his drinking friend's endurance. Jack grasped the bottle, but instead of drinking from it, he walked out of the door, and deliberately broke it over a log. Then, casting contemptuously upon the fragments a quantity of tobacco juice, he walked back to the door to give Smith a little wholesome advice. "Look here, 'Cracknose,' ef ye want ter larn the trick of drinkin' without gittin' set up, jest hump up yer back an' go down ter thet spring an' drink all ye kin. A little more of thet spring water inside an' outside will do ye a blamed sight more good than harm—ye hear?"

After delivering this temperance lecture, Jack thrust his hands into his pockets and walked unconcernedly off to the cook's shanty. Here, his first act was to divest himself of the paper collar. "These yar harness," he

remarked, "is likely ter raise collar biles on my neck."
Frank sat writing at the greasy table. It was always a wonder to the boys how he could write so many letters. To-day he was unusually busy. Perhaps the thought that this was Christmas day started many pleasant memories, or it may be that the journey of the night before had given him a pleasant theme. At any rate, he wrote on, covering page after page of paper. Jack watched him in silence for a while, and then broke in with : " Who ist ye write to ser much ? Hang me, ef ye don't sling more ink than a district school. Must hev more gals than a dry-goods clerk. I s'pose yer quite a master among the wimmin, ain't ye ?"

Frank was obliged to confess that his knowledge of the habits and feelings of the sex was somewhat limited.

"Wall, what I wuz thinkin' on wuz this. It kinder strikes me thet this yer doll-baby thet us two derned fools brung from Crystal last night is a blamed sight too slim fer sech a kid. I'd like ter git a doll-baby with fillygrees an' fixin's. Now, ef you knows any wimmin ez kin give us some p'ints on sech things, why can't ye jest line out the idees and draw out the p'ints. Then we kin kinder keep the thing hot, an' cook up some lie about meetin' Santa Claus agin an' gittin' another doll-baby out of him."

The cook came in just then, and Jack moved away as if ashamed of his errand. But Frank wrote the letter to his mother, not asking for " p'ints," but simply telling the story of how he acted as Santa Claus.

Two weeks had gone by since Santa Claus came wandering into Cooney Camp, and aired his "pickydillies" on the roof of Smith's cabin. The visit of the good old saint was almost forgotten by most of the boys. Many weighty things had happened in the mean time.

The little "kid" remembered him, however, though time had made sad havoc with the presents he left. The candy and orange had long since gone the way of their kind, and, revengeful as such things are apt to be, had made the little stocking-hanger sick in going. The jumping-jack had kicked his one sound leg completely off, and now viewed the world with a most melancholy countenance from the little shelf over the bed. Santa Claus himself could hardly have extracted a tune from the Jew's-harp, while "Cracknose" had accidently stepped on the tin whistle, and thus reduced its former note to a squeak. The poor little "doll-baby" had fallen and broken her nose off, much to the sorrow of the little "kid," who shed many tears over the misfortunes.

The worthy citizens of Cooney Camp were partaking of their early Sunday supper. The great mountains of beans and salt pork which had confronted them at the beginning of the meal had gone down before their active knives and forks.

But a silence, entirely new to the occasion, hung over the party. The faces of many of the men were dark with wrath.

The denizens of Cooney Camp felt that if any part of their etiquette was praiseworthy at all, it was their conduct at table. They fully believed in the physiological proposition that good nature and good digestion go hand in hand. A flow of delicate and refined wit could be always observed at their meals. Eating contests were largely encouraged, and the bare walls of the cook's shanty had looked down on many a gastronomic triumph.

The Sunday meal had heretofore been particularly lively. News of the week and many pleasant little anecdotes were always retailed for the benefit of the company.

But now the men sat with glum faces, and ate their meal in silence. They felt that they had been imposed upon. The shadow of a great sorrow had fallen upon them, and they had just received fresh and most direct evidence that this world is all a fleeting show.

Three days before, the supply teamster had brought into camp a box marked: "Miss Julia Watson, care of T. Smith, Cooney Camp."

The box was simple enough in its way, but it fell like a shell into the social life of the camp. The excitement was raised to fever-heat when the teamster informed the crowd that the owner of the box would follow it on Sunday.

"Miss Julia Watson, care of T. Smith!" The lumbermen studied the address carefully. Perhaps they expected to obtain some information from the shaky black letters written on the cover. The society of young and beautiful ladies was in active demand in Cooney Camp. By a series of original arguments and inferences, the lumbermen came to the conclusion that "Miss Julia Watson" must be both young and beautiful.

That she was young was sufficiently proved by the fact that she was a "miss." The genus "spinster" was entirely unknown to Cooney Camp.

I do not know how they proved the other quality. Perhaps there was something in the name. Ever since

Romeo risked his foolish neck climbing up to Juliet's window, the name of Julia has suggested both love and loveliness. The Cooney campers were probably not very thorough students of Shakespeare, but still there was something about the name that pleased them. Considerable curiosity was developed as to who "T. Smith" might be. This curiosity was, however, dispelled by the appearance of "Cracknose," who shouldered the box and started with it for his cabin. This action tended to spread abroad the fact that to the somewhat plebeian name of Smith he had joined the more æsthetic name of Theodore.

Not a word could "Cracknose" be induced to say in regard to the lady's appearance. She was simply a relative who was coming up, as he said, to see his "woman." There was a sly twinkle in his eye, unperceived by the boys, as he gravely announced that ef the boys wuz a mind ter hustle round an' kinder slick up, one on 'em mought stand a good show.

This information was enough to set the boys on their mettle at once. Such a washing and shaving and arraying in paper collars and clean shirts had never before been seen in camp. The visit of Santa Claus was nothing compared to this.

Barney and Bill even went so far as to engage in a fight for the possession of a paper collar. Though Barney at last secured possession of the coveted article, the black eye he received in obtaining it tended to neutralize the general effect it produced.

Nearly an hour before the time for the supply team, the boys gathered in front of the shanty, to give as much dignity as possible to the reception of the coming belle of Cooney Camp.

Some of the more poetic suggested the erection of

an arch of green boughs over the road, but the proposal did not meet with popular favor.

The air of restraint that hangs over every formal reception gradually wore away, and the free and easy style of Cooney Camp returned. The boys relieved the tedium of their waiting by betting upon the general appearance of the lady.

"I'll bet ye," began Tom, "thet she'll show up with yaller hair an' a pick-ed nose." There was some who differed with Tom. They seemed to be of the opinion that the young lady would appear with black hair. Others were positive that her nose would be short, or, as they graphically expressed it, "stubbed." It is my opinion that each one unconsciously described his own ideal of feminine loveliness. Tom's Venus-like description of "yaller hair an' a pick-ed nose" seemed to suit the majority.

Jack was the only man in camp who looked with undisguised contempt upon the whole affair.

Possibly he feared that the newcomer would absorb much of the attention now given to the little "kid." He was on the point of giving a sarcastic description of the charms of the newcomer, when the supply team came slowly under the two trees that stood where the road entered the forest. Sure enough, on the seat by the driver was a woman.

The expectant crowd waited till the wagon slowly rolled over the rough road and came to a halt before them.

The belle of Cooney Camp had come.

A thin woman, wrinkled and bent, sat on the seat of the wagon, and looked feebly about her. There was something pitiful and yet ludicrous in the sight.

The boys were too much overcome to speak. Bill

could only mutter, " Be we gonter start a bone yard up here?" Jack laughed at the discomfiture of the boys, and " Cracknose," with a " Howdy, *Aunt* Jule?" stepped forward and helped the old lady from the wagon.

Her greeting was characteristic. She looked at "Cracknose" critically for a moment, and then remarked thoughtfully, " It don't 'pear to me thet yer nose looks quite ser bad ez it did, though p'raps it is because I ain't gut my glasses on."

Smith received the delicate compliment in silence, and at once led the way to his own cabin.

It was a critical moment in the history of Cooney Camp. The boys were a little undecided what to do. Should they march in a body and mob the whole Smith family, or should they show their displeasure in some more forcible way?

Luckily, at this moment the cook blew a violent blast on the supper horn, and, impelled by the force of habit, the irate reception committee fell in and marched to the shanty.

As we before stated, the meal, so far as conversation was concerned, was a dire failure. It is hard, however, for a man with a full stomach to retain his anger long. The greatest hate and the most complete disappointment can seldom stand before a good dinner.

Toward the end of the meal the boys came to see something of the joke of the affair, and one or two even ventured to laugh with Jack.

They were about attacking an instalment of dried-apple pies, when "Cracknose" came in with a small package in his hand.

" The ole lady," he stated, " hed this yer bundle gin her ter be brought out, jest ez the team started.

'Pears like it must be fer you," and he handed the package to Frank. Then, seeing the angry eyes of the crowd fixed upon him, he rightly inferred that his presence could be easily dispensed with, and slipped out of the door.

Frank looked at the bundle curiously. It had come all the way from Boston. The boys watched him as he cut the string and took off the paper.

"I 'low somebody's sent ye a box of cigars. *I* smoke onct or twict a year," suggested Bill.

The paper taken off disclosed a long pasteboard box. Frank wonderingly removed the cover, and revealed to the astonished eyes of the crowd a beautiful doll dressed in the very height of fashion, and apparently smiling sweetly at the rough faces gathered about it.

A little folded slip of paper lay in the box. Frank opened it, and read : " For the little girl in the camp who prayed Santa Claus to send her a dolly." The little one's prayer had been heard. A far gentler Santa Claus than he who toiled wearily into camp on Christmas morning had been commissioned to fill the little stocking again.

Hundreds of miles from the rough camp the story of the little "kid" had touched a woman's heart. The "wimmen" had sent Jack "p'ints" with good effect. Perhaps even while the little "kid" was praying in the rough cabin, she who had sent the doll was listening to her own little ones as they sleepily murmured the same little prayer. Perhaps she sat watching them after they had fallen asleep, not with tearful eyes like her who watched beside that little one in the forest, but with a happy, thankful heart. It may be that He, who heard both prayers, answered by moving her to fill the little blue stocking. Perhaps all our prayers are answered thus. Would that we could believe it! Would that we all could have the faith of that little child!

When the box was opened, there was an astonished silence for a moment. Such a sight had never before been seen in Cooney Camp. The doll was taken out and carefully handed about for inspection.

In the bottom of the box were a few little picture-books. These were seized by the more literary members of the crowd, who explained the pictures for the benefit of the less educated. The big men were like children with a new toy.

"I'll be hanged," shouted Tom, "ef there ain't a picter of a young lad ez hez clumb up ter the top of a high pump fer ter drink out frum the nizzle."

Sure enough they could all see it.

"But," put in Barney, "do ye mind the other young lad with his holt on the handle unbeknownst ter the other?" And the crowd laughed in great glee at the thought of the ducking the first boy would receive.

But the doll, after all, was the great centre of attraction. The little red dress and cape, the blue eyes and the hair, to use Jack's expression, "kinder gut away with a carpet store."

After the toy had been handed about for a while, Jack suggested that it was time to "call it in."

He placed it carefully in the box, and announced his intention of taking it over to the "kid" at once.

"Ye see," he argued, "I hev ben swappin' lies with the kid afore, an' I kin kinder keep the thing hot. I'll tell the story, an' don't one of ye say a word or I'll lick him."

No one was disposed to question Jack's right to the position of spokesman.

Free thought and free speech are two great elements of our national freedom; but when such a fist as Jack's is held in front of him, one is willing to look upon them as the fox regarded the grapes.

With Jack at their head, the men adjourned to Smith's cabin. Those who could, crowded into the room, while the others looked in at the door and windows.

The antiquated "miss" had evidently just been giving the family an account of her journey.

Perhaps she looked upon the sudden arrival of the delegation as something in the light of a popular reception extended by the citizens of Cooney Camp to her.

In order the more fully to show her appreciation of the good-will of the company, she made haste to put on her "glasses," and through them she viewed Jack with undisguised admiration, which tended to embarrass him exceedingly.

The admiring glance of a lady's eye was enough by itself; but when it was magnified by passage through the convex lens of a pair of "glasses," to use his own expression, it "gut away" with him.

He began his remarks by saying that he 'lowed he warn't so derned small thet it tuck four eyes ter see him. Ef he wuz, he'd grow a little.

This delicate intimation had the desired effect. The "glasses" were removed.

Jack then proceeded:

"Ye see when I ketched this yer Santy Claus on the ruff here a couple of weeks ago, I didn't say nuthin', but it seemed to me thet the doll-baby he sent wuz pretty blamed slim. He had a big bag on his back, an' I see him sortin' out his truck. Thar wuz lots of big doll-babies thar with rale hair an' all the fillygrees. T'warn't none of my bizness, but I sez ter myself, ef I ever see him agin, I'll jest tech him up a bit. I wuz out in the woods ter-day, an', hang me, ef I didn't come plumb onter him. I knowed him by his picky-dilly pants. I jest went up an' sez, ' Hev yer gut any terbacker?' He sed he had, an' opens his bag ter find some. When he opens it I see inside ez fine a doll-baby ez ever wuz growed. I made up an' told him jest how the thing stood, an', I'll be hanged, ef he didn't do the square thing. He jest yanked out thet doll-baby an' gin it ter me. He sed he hed a long walk afore him, an' kinder asked me ef I wouldn't brung it round. I told him I would, an', hang me, ef it ain't here," and Jack placed the box in the little " kid's" hands, and then deliberately walked out of the cabin.

Most of the crowd followed him, but one or two, anxious to see what the little " kid" would do, peeped in at the window.

The little one opened the box with wondering eyes, which grew wider at the sight of the doll.

As a woman takes her baby to her breast, so the little " kid" gathered the toy in her arms, and hugged it as she rocked back and forth in her chair.

At last she looked up and saw on the shelf over the bed the mutilated face of the other dolly looking sorrowfully upon her. She laid the larger doll on the floor while she climbed on the bed and took the smaller one from its place. When she sat down again, she held both of them.

Just after dark, Jack came in again, pretending that he wished to see Smith about an axe.

The little girl sat with tears in her eyes, looking

wistfully at the new dolly perched upon the wall above the looking-glass.

The "belle" noticed Jack's look of wonder, and made haste to explain.

"Ye see, I kinder thought the little gal might sile the doll's dress, an' then it looked kinder pert on the wall, so I thought I'd stick it up there, an' let her set an' look at it."

For a moment Jack was speechless with anger. Then he took down the doll and gave it to the little girl.

Then, actually shaking his fist in the face of the old lady, he fairly roared with more force than elegance: "Ef yer stick thet doll-baby up thar agin, I'll wring yer neck!"

The doll never went to the wall again.

When the child went to bed that night she took her dolly with her. Just as the little eyes were closing in sleep, she murmured half to herself, "Dod bess Santy Caus for sendin' my dolly."

And Santa Claus will be blessed.

I wish I could close this story by telling how this little incident started a permanent reform in camp. Most stories end in this way, but mine cannot.

Jack and Bill and Tom and all the rest went back to their old ways. They drank and swore and fought as hard as ever, and yet I cannot help thinking that they were all made better and purer in some way by that little girl's prayer and its answer.

The oftener the tender, diviner chords of our being are touched, the more easily will they stir in sympathy for others.

The little "kid" will not forget that Christmas eve, nor the present Santa Claus sent by Jack.

Ah! if we only knew the pleasure and comfort we might give by a single kind word or look or generous act! If we only knew of the thousands of human beings who only need the kindly and gentle impulse to lead them to purer and better lives, we might still act a Santa Claus, and make life one perpetual Christmas, more merry even than the celebration at Cooney Camp.

But we cannot, for our eyes are blinded.

Everybody thanked George Hackmatack when he was done.

Every one felt how exactly the story belonged to their party, blocked in as they were.

Old lumbermen were there, on their way down from the Rockies. They saw how true the little story is to man and to nature.

And I dare not say how many of the women were crying.

Mr. Van Sandfoord gave time enough for talk, for questions and for sympathy, and then pretended to consult the great placard of the programme, of which the first sheet was pinned beside him, big enough for those that ran to read.

"Mrs. Fréchette will favor us with a ballad."

The little woman did not flinch an instant.

"The committee had no right to ask me for an original ballad," said she. "I never write ballads, and Tom does not. But I will sing an old Yankee ballad, which I learned on Thanksgiving day from a real Mayflower girl. She says the people in Plymouth County—I think that is the place—knew what the time was some two hundred years ago or less. You must all join in the chorus."

And with great spirit she sang :

" 'Twas up to Uncle Tracy's,
    The fifth of November,
Last Thanksgiving night,
    As I very well remember :
And there we had a frolic,
    A frolic, indeed,
And drank several glasses
    Of good anise-seed.

" And there was Parson Holmes,
    And there was Perez Drew,
And there was Seth Gilbert,
    And Seth Thomas, too ;
And there were too many,
    Too many for to name,
And by and by I'll tell you how
    We carried on the game.

" We carried on the game
    Till 'twas late in the night—
There was one pretty girl
    And she lost her eye-sight.
No wonder—no wonder—
    No wonder, indeed,
For she drank three full glasses
    Of good anise-seed."

She sang the quaint old air so merrily and she commanded the rest so instinctively that they caught it quickly, and sang the last half of each verse with her.

Amid general laughing she turned to Mr. Decker, and said :

" That is the way your Yankee ancestors kept Thanksgiving, Mr. Decker, before Nahum Barrow's time. I do not know what anise-seed is. It shows how things are improved, that I do not."

And so they hummed the air, and taught each other the words, till Hector, in his stentorian way, shouted: "Number three."

AN ORATION BY MR. MENET.

"I am a wretched public speaker," said Mr. Menet, "when my wife is not by me to prompt me. So soon as I saw the programme I was frightened, and have been ever since. I once delivered a Fourth-of-July oration in Spanish to my workmen. But last night I found, first, that I could not alter the allusions to independence in time, and, next, that I had forgotten the oration. So I throw myself on your mercy, and ask leave to tell a story."

They all cried, "Story! story! story!"

"Well," said Menet, laughing, "next I thought to tell really a curious story of something which happened at a Christmas dinner I was at in Paris."

Here all four of the palace ladies showed danger signals; for they all blushed scarlet, conscious that they knew that story well. But Menet did not notice, and went on.

"But that is really rather too personal. And so I have been mean enough to go forward to the newsboy's box. I gave him a bit of money, and he let me dig there. I mention this because I scorn to lie, and I have pre-empted that box, and no one else is to burrow there. I shall have the pleasure to read you a story called "Christmas at Valley Forge," which I found in his box, and I venture to say to Mr. Decker that the hero is not my grandfather.

So Mr. Menet read, and read very well, from an old *Frank Leslie*, the story of

CHRISTMAS AT VALLEY FORGE.

THANKSGIVING DAY.

"There," said Elam Ford, swinging himself down from a heavy wooden table on which he had been standing, "I'll stump all the dogs in the haven to push her open now!" and the squad of lazy soldiers around him rang applause and approval of the success of an enterprise for which none but Elam had the spirit.

"Elam means to have one hull turkey for himself, and he's afraid the dogs will get part of his share."

"Or the cats!" growled another of the squad, and a general laugh saluted the jest, which contained an allusion to some wretched mess anecdote.

Nobody laughs so easily as boys or girls off duty.

"Well," said Elam, "I said last night, I did, ses I, when old spitfire there came sneaking up from the cellar, and poked his nose in, and then came in himself, I says, says I, I did, I'll be darned if I don't get the trunnion of the gun we bust, and hang it fur a weight to that 'ere door, and I'll be darned if I lie here all night and have dogs and cats and weasels and kittens and puppies smellin' over my bunk, cos Enos or Jotham or Micah or any of you fellers was so stupid you could not latch the cellar-door. I said I would, and I've gone and done it."

And with one last loving touch he tested his handiwork.

He swung the door open, and the pulley weight of the heavy trunnion banged it to with a force that shook the whole cabin from ground-sill to roof-tree.

It was a wretched hole at the best. It was a log cabin, which this squad of men had built for themselves as the winter came on.

The English army, under Howe, was taking its ease in Philadelphia; and Washington on the Wissahickon Creek and the Schuylkill River was watching them, and occasionally making a stroke at a foraging party.

The particular party with which we are concerned had been sent up to inspect a ford of the larger river, and, eventually, to throw up a redoubt which should command it.

They had made themselves as comfortable as they could by building this cabin for their quarters.

In the hole below, dignified by the name of "cellar," or "suller," as the reader chooses to take the English or the Yankee pronunciation, they had such stores of potatoes, of cabbages, and of salt pork as the commissariat or their own vigorous foraging provided.

Bunks, in which they slept, were arranged around the walls; a fixed table with benches on each side occupied the middle of the cabin, and a fire, which would have served Cyclops, blazed at one end.

"We can't do nothin' more about dinner," said Elam, who was evidently the most energetic person in the party, "till Siah's off and Michael."

And after looking out at the open door, he turned back a little dissatisfied.

"In theyre, pinkin' and foolin', 'n powderin' their hair, most likely, for the general's party, and the womenfolks there. There's that poor mare looks 'zif she'd freeze, while Michael's puttin' more pomatum on his queue."

Another general guffaw saluted this irreverent allusion to an officer.

For "Josiah" and "Michael," as Elam called them, were the captain and lieutenant in command of the outpost.

They were old companions in school and in play of the men whom they were supposed to command.

It was by a severe strain that the traditional decencies of English and German armies had been so far preserved that they had a different cabin from those occupied by the men.

It was with the greatest difficulty that the men were held to any tokens of outward respect on drill or parade.

When the boys were by themselves the officers were plain "Michael" and "Josiah" again.

To-day the officers were going to eat their Thanksgiving dinner with General Knox at his headquarters, and at this moment the mice were waiting for the cats to go away, that their own Thanksgiving might begin.

The Thanksgiving day was, in fact, appointed a week later than that.

They had not to wait long.

In a few minutes the jingle of sleigh bells told that the toilets of the officers were completed, and in a moment more Captain Josiah Marvin knocked, and, without waiting an answer, came in on the men.

The tokens of respect which met him were of the slightest.

But such tokens there were.

"Well, boys," he said, "it's a spare Thanksgiving any of us will have at best; but I've brought you over all the rum we have left, and if you take it all—it will not hurt you—you're welcome. You got the big rooster? I wish there were anything else. But you must make the junk do for filling. You Cape Codders, I suppose, like a cape turkey best. A pleasant night to you all. You know Silas is on duty. Don't make them wait for the relief; but I shall be back before then. Good-night to you."

"Good-night, good-night, sir." And the captain joined his companions, and was off.

No sooner had the door closed than Elam swung back his cellar-door and vanished, only to reappear with both hands full, and a very droll imitation of the captain's manner.

"Wal, boys, it's a spare Thanksgiving any of us will have, at best," he said. "But I've brought you this old gobbler, and these three little biddies, and this here goose, and a pair of ducks, that was all strutting and parading last evenin' down to the old Dutchman's at the crossing. The Dutchman did not know it was Thanksgiving day, so he did not know what they was good for. But I know'd mighty well, only I thort I'd let him keep 'em for us till we was ready. Now, here's my ramrod, and that goes through gobblers and quack-quacks. Who gives his ramrod for little quack here? not so little either, and for young cut-cut ke dar cut?"

There was no lack of ramrods, nor of cooks to tend the roast.

By preconcerted invitation, the men from the captain's quarters and those from another cabin in the hollow soon joined. And what with the captain's rum and old Freinhardt's poultry, the revel of the Thanksgiving evening went forward with as much plenty, if not as much elegance, as would have been found that night in any household in New England.

"Half an hour yet before the relief," cried Mr.

Micah Stearns. "There'll be no need of turning out till then. Gin us another song, Dot."

And Dot wet his whistle for the tenth time, and sang a camp ballad.

A heavy knock at the door broke in on the closing words of the song, and again Captain Marvin threw it open.

"That's right, boys; make a jolly time of it. I looked in to see if you were all ready for the relief. But I see nobody's asleep here."

And he did his best not to see the carcasses of the turkey, the ducks, and the chickens, which lay in horrible disorder on the table.

Elam, with a wholly unnatural effort at military etiquette, sprang to his feet, and saluted. "All right, captain. I command the relief myself, and I'm sober —sober—sober, captain, as the clock."

"I see you are," said the captain, laughing, and turning away as quickly as he could from the scene he was sorry he had looked in upon.

"Lights and fires must be out after the relief marches, boys. Parade at sunrise, you know," and he was gone.

Alas! the provant was all gone, too; the result of Elam's injudicious foraging. The last drop of rum had gone to wet Micah Stearn's whistle, and the company were fain to break up, when a bugle from below announced that the officer on duty expected the relief.

The men put on such apologies for overcoats as they had.

The guests of the cabin bade good-night.

Elam gave the word, "Forward, march," and the Thanksgiving revel was ended.

The morning parade of the company was steady enough. It was not till Saturday morning that compensation came. We are never so stiff the day after a rough ride as we are on the second day.

On Saturday morning every man who could be spared from the little outpost was marched a mile and a half or more to brigade headquarters. Nobody knew why. The men, as they marched, even guessed that some sudden dash at one of Howe's outposts might be proposed. But nobody could guess why the regular arrangements for the reliefs and duty on the picket-lines were broken up. Broken up they were ; and, if anybody had noticed, the whole party of Thanksgiving revellers were present at the parade.

The parade went off sufficiently well, though some people's hands were cold with handling musket-butts in the frosty air. But, after the parade, the men were held while a brigade general order was read. The major-general commanding that division had been appealed to by old Freinhardt, whose poultry-yard had been stripped. It was at the very moment when they were deciding at headquarters whether the whole army should not be brought up for the winter to Valley Forge. It was particularly desirable, therefore, that the few farmers in that region should be conciliated. And so it was that one example of great severity had to be made, of the frolic which might have been winked at otherwise, of Elam Ford and the other boys. Much of this was set forth in the rather cumbrous general order, which ended by ordering six of those soldiers under arrest for a week, and by directing that Sergeant Ford should be reduced to the ranks,

and be kept under arrest for a month at that. The
order went so far as to say that but for this act of dis-
obedience he would have been promoted to a lieutenancy on the first of the year. Now, a lieutenancy was
exactly what Elam had been looking forward to, with
good reason, ever since they had crossed the North
River.

The rage of the whole company knew no bounds.
Marvin and Guthrie, who were both very fond of
Elam, were as sorry as anybody could be, and had
been at work, if he had but known it, all the day before, pleading with the colonel, and been doing their
best with General Glover at brigade headquarters.
But nothing would do. The Dutchman must be conciliated. The whole army was probably to move at once
up the river and take post at Valley Forge, and there
must be an example made, and poor Elam was the
example. Sour and cross, the company marched
back to its quarters, the men under arrest following
behind. Sour and cross they spent the days, not to
say weeks, that followed. When the whole army
marched across to join them, from the Wissahickon
and up from below, that changed the external of things
a little. But what are the externals? At heart, every
man, whether under arrest or no, was enraged. All
the revellers were as guilty as Elam, and those not
punished used to go to the captain and lieutenant,
Marvin and Guthrie, and say so, with a freedom
which in any other service would have been severely
punished, but which in the democratic New England
regiments of those days was universal. Yet Marvin
and Guthrie could not even whisper that the punishment had been inflicted in face of their eager protest.
The tie which held privates with the army was none

too strong at best, and it was not for them to loosen the cords of discipline.

Readers must not suppose that these men who were under arrest were chained, like Baron Trenck, by wrists and ankles, to blocks of stone in underground dungeons. The resources of Valley Forge were not equal to such confinement, had there been cruelty enough to desire it, as there was not. It was expected that they would report at the guard-house several times in a day. It was also understood that they would not appear at guard-mountings and parade. But not a man of them even affected to be pleased at this relaxation from duty. They were disgraced before the brigade, and it was a disgrace they did not deserve, they said. As for military duty, that was what they had come for, and they thought it no hardship. Indeed, with the scanty resources of their outpost, the poor occupation of drill and guard-mounting was more a pleasure than toil.

They hung about grumbling. Elam's punishment lasted three weeks longer than the others. For a month he had nothing to do. To pass away the time, he amused himself with old Freinhardt's children, not because they were his enemy's children, but because they were somebody's children. Not one of Freinhardt's family could speak a word of English, and Elam did not know that he could speak a word of German. But he soon found out that "come here," with a red apple presented by the speaker, meant much the same to a little German tot, as if he had said "komm hier," and he and the army of children became good friends. The heavy teams and the artillery sleds hauling stones up from the Schuylkill had made a very tempting coast, and the bigger boys had availed themselves of the facilities thus given to make a crowd of what the Canadians call "toboggins," and of little "jumpers," to borrow a Virginian phrase. But Elam and Micah astonished them by a Yankee combination of two very large sleds, in the genuine pattern of the largest of "double-runners" of the New England hills. And when a party of twenty were piled upon this craft, and it shot down near half a mile upon the frozen river, even grumpy old Freinhardt himself would take out his eternal pipe long enough to express his approbation. There was not a woman in his household who did not, sooner or later, take a ride down the hill on the "John Hancock," as the rude vehicle was called. And Gottfried, the big boy, whom Elam secretly meant to enlist into his company in the spring, was soon as skilful as Elam himself in the mysteries of steering. For other amusement, Elam had skating, in which he was an adept, from old Merrimac experience, and Gottfried stealthily purveyed a pair of Dutch skates from the garret of Freinhardt's house to the soldier's cabin for Elam's personal use. Little did the "old Dutchman," as he was always called, though he never was in Holland—little did he suppose that his arch-enemy was gliding on his own fleet irons, when he had to grumble out his confession that the Yankee's skates seemed to answer as well as if they had been made in Amsterdam.

None the less, in all these sports was Elam disgusted; a little disgusted with himself, perhaps, but thoroughly enraged with his colonel and with the brigadier. Such was his condition at bottom. Superficially, at top, his rage was that he should be "fooling away his time." For to the genuine Yankee, eager of purpose, and with a quite definite conviction that Almighty God has left to him, personally, the greater share of the direction of the world, mere recreation, after the third day, always becomes an insufferable bore. He despises any person whom he sees engaging in it. He despises himself equally, if circumstances have forced him into it.

Meanwhile the entire neighborhood of Valley Forge had assumed unwonted activity. The whole army under Washington had been ordered thither, to hold a position where General Howe, the English commander, could be watched through the winter. Axes were served out, and heavy timber, as the men were to build cabins for themselves. The cabin which Elam's men had built some weeks before, when they were first bidden to hold this bridge over the Schuylkill, became a pattern much studied and much admired. Wood there was in plenty, for the hills were covered with it. But there was little plenty of anything else. Still the army was in good spirits, and did not yet know what was before it, as that weary winter should pass by. The regiment to which Marvin's company belonged was already so well hutted, that no great change was made in their quarters, and Elam and his companions were free to give such counsel and assistance as they might to working parties who had not had their experience.

SURPRISE.

So matters ground along for the first few weeks of poor Elam Ford's disgrace. The other privates tried to be specially kind to him, but their clumsy efforts seemed only to remind him of his misfortune. His superior officers in the immediate command, Marvin and Guthrie, also tried to be kind to him, but their kindness he could and would resent almost as an insult. Not that he once suspected Captain Marvin as having "peached" upon him. He knew perfectly well that it was by other testimony that he had been convicted at brigade headquarters of the onslaught on the Dutchman's henyard. But he was angry that these men, who were of his own time, old schoolmates and allies, had not used their influence to save him. For little did he know that they had both strained their means of grace to the very utmost.

At last the month of "arrest" was nearly over. But the last days were, perhaps, the worst of all. Every cabin near him was finished, and he had no excuse for lending a hand among working parties. The very worst day came when Marvin and Guthrie again ordered round the sleigh, which was the only vehicle for the use of the whole post, and with the poor old mare that had taken them to Thanksgiving at General Glover's, drove off to a grand Christmas dinner, which was given by Smallwood, of the Maryland line. Elam was quite alone as he saw them go. All of his messmates were on picket duty that day. He would have been were it not for his cursed arrest. He crawled up into his bunk, pulled over him the wretched blanket which was his only night covering, turned his face from the light, and did his best to sleep.

He had not lain there five minutes before the door of the cabin was flung open, and, to Elam's surprise, a crowd of men thronged in, voluble with oaths and ejaculations. But an instant taught him. As he lay he could see that these were a squad of English dragoons, who had stealthily crossed the little patch from the woods behind, where they had been waiting till the detail of Americans should move down the hill, and now, so soon as their backs were turned, had taken possession of the cabin.

"All gone!" said the officer in command, with more oaths than need be repeated here. "So much the better. Every shot saved is so much time gained. A good fire they have left us, no thanks to them. William, take the boys down the hill. Ferguson will stop every blackguard in the other barrack here; do you join his men at the fork; wait for the party of the Queen's at the barn in the hollow, and I will find you there. I'll just warm my fingers here, and make sure about the lane road."

As he spoke he drew a bit of tracing paper from his pocket, opened it upon the table, and began to study the map upon it, as he clapped his cold hands together. The subaltern touched his hat, and withdrew the men.

The orders given were enough to show to Elam in an instant what was the design; and a design wonderfully well laid it was. Relying on the Christmas festivities of the Pennsylvania brigades, as confidently as Washington, a year before, had relied on those of the Hessians, the English colonel who had, by a bold push, ridden round the American army with two companies of dragoons, had broken them into small squads, who had worked their way through the woods, and were now on the eve of re-union quite inside the only picket lines held by Americans on that side of Valley Forge which was most distant from Philadelphia. Had the roads been hard, a ten minutes' gallop would take them to the very house where thirty of the most distinguished officers of Washington's right wing were dining. As it was, they were expecting to arrive there just after dark, and in the confusion of such an onslaught they would have a good chance to make prizes. All this passed through Elam Ford's mind in an instant. He sickened as he thought of the treachery which had taught them where to strike the blow. He did not dare to move lest he should lose every chance of rendering service. Yet he should die, he knew, if he did nothing.

From this distress, however, a single minute relieved him. The English captain, perfectly unconscious, in the darkness of the cabin, that he was not alone, turned to the fire to warm his hands over the embers, and, lifting a heavy log, flung it across the bricks which served for andirons. Availing himself of the noise and the movement of the other, Elam turned instantly on his elbow, saw the situation at once, sprang from the bunk upon his feet behind the other, and, taking him wholly unawares, pushed him down, as he bent over, into the very fireplace which he was feeding. Then, without pausing a moment, Elam drew open the cellar-door, sprang down the rough steps into the darkness, gave one wrench at this ladder, enough to loosen it and throw it upon the ground, and then pushed open a bulkhead at a passage where they were used to haul in such stores as were kept there. He could hear the oaths and cries of the officer above him, and he knew that at best his time was very short. He was even glad to see no movement at the other cabin and to hear no sound from below, although these were indications that the raiding party was already some minutes on its way toward the quarry.

He was closely pursued, as he knew that he should be, but, fortunately for him, the pursuit was arrested as suddenly as it began. The English captain recovered himself from the fall, not without scorchings and burnings, which at another time he would have thought horrible, but which at this instant did not hinder him for a moment. The bang of Elam's door had taught him, only too well, the way of his escape, and it required but a minute to find, in the gathering darkness, the trick of opening it. He swung it back, and boldly sprang down as the other had done, but to a longer leap. He fell, badly bruised, upon the rough step-ladder, and as he tried to extricate himself found his hands and arms fettered by the accident that his dragoon's cloak, trailing behind him, had caught upon something in the floor above, and was already firmly secured in the heavy swing of Elam's door. At first the poor captain had a feeling that above and below some bear or panther had pounced upon him, for the English army was full of imagined terrors of the wilderness; and in a dark hole like this, alone on a winter's night, even a man of his experience recurred to the stories which told of them. But in an instant more he made sure that nobody was pinioning him but himself. He did not, however, so quickly find how he was to be unpinioned. His left arm, which lay under him, refused so stubbornly to come to the rescue, that he was afraid it was broken. His right arm was all twisted out of its place by the tight strain of the cloak upon it, and when he brought round the burnt fingers to the clasp which bound this at the throat, it seemed only too clear that this was in one of those tangles which even the saints call "infernal," and which no power which those poor blistered fingers could bring upon it could make it yield.

With every effort which he made to rise upon his knees, the steps of the ladder under him seemed to trip and tumble him over, and every such effort taught him that his left arm was broken or dislocated at the shoulder. Once and again, indeed, in such efforts he thought he should be choked by the bearing of the throat-latch, which would not be undone. He was in utter darkness, because Elam had closed the opening through which he had rushed into the open air. It was thus that the unfortunate officer lost the precious minutes in which alone his pursuit of Elam would have been effected.

These minutes, indeed, were very few. Before two minutes were past Elam Ford was half a mile away, safe on the firm ice of the Schuylkill. If, as he left the cabin, he had the slightest doubt as to his course, that doubt was solved for him as, with his first glance around, he saw the bulky form of the " John Hancock" by the roadway, where Gottfried and the others had left her when summoned home by the horn which called them to their Christmas dinner. Had Pegasus, full-winged, stood before him or a champing war horse pawed to do him service, Elam would not have been so well pleased. For, indeed, here was a charger whose paces he understood better than those of hippogriff or destrier. In half a minute he had drawn the "John Hancock" to the brow of the hill. Less than half a minute was enough to roll and throw upon the hinder sled a heavy log which the men had hauled thus far to cut and split for firing. Then Elam started the huge machine, ran an instant by its side, flung himself upon the foremost sled with the two steering spikes which had lain upon it, and with a speed such as racehorse never rivalled dashed down the icy hill.

Colonel Bedford's line of mounted pickets had been thrown out with true military precision, to make sure that no straggler of the rebels carried any news of the English advance down his well-worn way. In that line of pickets was a Yorkshireman, as near-sighted as the average Yorkshireman, and not badly mounted. He sat upon his horse, wondering how long it might be before the main party should return, and with sufficient care watching the roadway in the gathering twilight.

The sun was already down. But what care could arrest the flight or the headlong charge of the well-directed "John Hancock"? Nay, what horse of the best training would stand without flinching the sight of such an apparition? As Elam dashed by on his lightning track, the trooper's horse shied wildly, and, although the man fired his pistol, he fired it at nothing, and the only effect of the discharge was to startle the American pickets, unconscious till this moment that they had been wholly outflanked, and that an enemy was inside their lines.

Elam Ford rushed on, on his unobstructed way. From the crest where he started to the smooth ice of the river is, perhaps, half a mile. And for such a vehicle, well steered, thirty seconds was enough for the descent. Plunging upon the glaring ice, Elam threw his whole weight upon the steering pike, which he drove into the smooth surface on his larboard side. The huge sledge obeyed its helm, and after one critical moment, when it seemed tottering as if to turn over, it dashed down the river. It shot forward nearly half a mile more, before it lost the impetus of the hill. So soon as the motion slackened, Elam drew himself up, loosened from one of the posts of the sledge a pair of skates which hung there, and before the "John Hancock" had well stopped, he had strapped them upon his feet and was ready for his further journey.

Just as he stood on the ice against the white slope of the hill, he saw another moving figure coming fearlessly toward him. Elam could not avoid him if he would, and in an instant was glad he had made no effort to, when he recognized the friendly voice of Gottfried. "I shouldn't been more tickled," said Elam afterward, "had it been an angel from heaven." To send Gottfried to the guard-house above, and warn Lieutenant Faunce of the enemy's position, while he himself carried the alarm to the Christmas party of officers below—if yet there was time—this was his effort. But how to send a messenger who does not speak one's language. Elam seized that intuition of speaking loudly and slowly, which has served so many wayfaring men, though fools, since the Tower of Babel. He pointed to the block-house, which was full in sight, though near a mile up the river, and cried : " Faunce, Faunce !" " Ja wohl, ja wohl," cried the willing Gottfried. " Faunce, Faunce, a hundred troopers !" screamed poor Elam so loudly that even Faunce himself could have heard had he been listening. " Ja wohl, ja wohl," said Gottfried again. " Hundert trupper, hundert trupper, ich verstehe." " Smallwood," screamed Elam, pointing now down the river. " Ja wohl, Smallwood," said the other, to whom that general's name and person were perfectly well known, and had Elam written him a despatch of forty folios he would not have understood better than he did that a force of a hundred cavalrymen were threatening Smallwood, and that he was to carry that news to Faunce's little outpost. He dashed up the river faster than a bird. Never had he skated on such an errand or with such a motive. The little mile between him and the outpost was nothing. In as little time as it takes to describe it, he had passed over the distance on the river, and, as he clambered up the low bank, was within call of Faunce's puzzled men. The bugler had already given the alarm. The pickets were falling in from every side, leaving only a line of observation. Lieutenant Faunce himself, perplexed, ran down the bank to receive Gottfried's message. The boy was too well known in the whole company to be doubted. There were men who well understood him when he spoke in his own language, and his perfectly coherent story was enough to induce the lieutenant to lead the greater part of his detachment, by the quickest pace possible, through the heavy snow by the river road direct to the Forge in the valley.

A LITTLE DINNER PARTY.

Meanwhile, at the little central village of the improvised town, General Smallwood had collected his Christmas party. It was made up on no principle of rank ; but, by his inviting gentlemen whom he had met in the severe service in the last year, whatever the State Line to which they belonged, Smallwood pleased himself with the thought that he was thus bringing together officers from all parts of the country. Marvin had been his especial favorite since he covered the rear in the sharp skirmish in Greenwood the day of the fatal battle of Brooklyn. And Smallwood was never more pleased—though he was certainly surprised —than when the young New Englander told him, as he entered the room, that this was the first Christmas dinner he had ever eaten with the recollection that it was Christmas day.

General Smallwood's satisfaction was complete when, just as they were to sit down, one of his aides came clattering up to the door with a message from the "marquis," as Lafayette was everywhere called, to say that he was unexpectedly at liberty, and would accept General Smallwood's invitation, which he had before declined. The table, served for thirty in the long log cabin, which had been run out behind the inn to serve as a dining-room, was readily arranged for the distingushed guest and De Kalb whom he had brought with him. The varied uniforms of the different State "Lines" had not yet all given way to the blue and buff. Blue, white, and green varied the long line of the table ; and even the red coat, which was in general the sign of an enemy, appeared in two instances as the uniform of Morgan's horse. Never had a more distinguished party gathered under the newly-baptized American flag.

Marvin winced a little as Smallwood turned to him, as soon as he began to carve a twenty-pound turkey. "Marvin," said he, " we have not let Glover's line eat all the gobblers for their Thanksgiving. We have a few more left in the plantations, and they do say there are some of the blue hen's chickens at the other end of the table."

The Thanksgiving order of the day at Glover's brigade had become camp talk.

"I am afraid," said Marvin, "that the Maryland turkeys are better than those they bring us from Cape Cod."

The answer pleased the Marylander, who explained to Lafayette, who sat at his right, that his wife had sent a special express to camp, which had arrived only the night before, to supply the stores for the full feast which was before them. But it was impossible for the genial Marylander to understand the feeling—closer than feudal feeling—which bound the New England captain to his privates. And little did he think that in his joke he had renewed the only bitter sting which that day could have for the brave young officer of whom he was so fond.

This little story must not stop to tell of the gay talk of that gay dinner. Lafayette told bright stories of London life, even of the very men who were in front of them in Philadelphia. He spoke grammatical English with a fascinating French accent and an occasional blunder in idiom which gave a zest to his slow narration, whose enforced delay contrasted oddly with the eagerness of the flow of his thought. Even De Kalb told stories from the French mess-rooms. The Southern gentlemen had negro stories, Indian stories, and no end of rallying of the New Englanders who knew so little of Christmas.

The New Englanders were not behind in pity for men who had never heard of Thanksgiving. Everybody who had been within a hundred miles of Trenton and the crash on Rahl the year before, fought that battle over again, and gayer and gayer sounded the talk and brighter and more joyous was the song in German, in French, and in English, as the afternoon passed, and the sun went down.

Lafayette had just begun singing, to the amusement of everybody, some new French words to the air of "*Mironton, mironton, mirontaine,*" when, at a word from Smallwood, a white-haired old negro—the same who had conveyed the poultry from his plantation—entered at the head of a black procession, who bore three extemporized chandeliers made from barrel-hoops wreathed in evergreen and tallow-dips already lighted.

"Yes, Zeno, you may stand on the table," said Smallwood, laughing. And the old man mounted with dignity, and hung his elegant circle of light upon a hook in the rafter already provided. He took a second hoop from the man behind him, and the gentlemen were fairly clapping him, in laughing praise of his dexterity, when the farther door of the dining-room was flung open, and at the same moment a bugle outside sounded "To horse," in a strain which every man there understood perfectly.

Elam Ford sprang in at the open door. He was, of course, instantly recognized by Marvin and Guthrie. "Belford's horse—a party of two companies—on the river road!"

"General," said Elam, even in that moment reporting with military precision to his own brigadier-general, Glover, "they have dodged our pickets. They met at the hollows and are coming down the river road to this place. I have heard the order." And outside, as he spoke, Harry Lee's bugle-man sounded "To horse, to horse, to horse!"

The gay party melted from the scene, no man knew how. Every man of them, of course, was dressed according to the old rule of chivalry, which required that a gentleman should always be ready to mount and to ride as for his life. Windows and doors flew open, and in a moment more there was no man at the gayly-lighted board.

Each officer was searching for a horse and on his way to his command.

Light-horse Harry himself sprang on a white horse he found at the door—he knew not whose—and rode to the side of his bugler, who was till sounding "To horse, to horse!"

Elam Ford, as he left the table, seized the American flag which hung over the host's chair. Had Elam known it, it had been embroidered in silk by Mrs. Smallwood's friends on the "Eastern shore." Elam thrust the steering pike, which he still held, through the silken folds, and ran out to the road, which was almost as light as day, from Zeno's blazing candles within the open room.

"Rally on the colors!" cried Elam, lustily, "rally on the colors! Yes, boys, form by twos on the colors," speaking in the language of tactics long since forgotten. "Form on the colors—form on the colors—for God's sake form on the colors! Where are you going, Butternut? Form on the colors."

"Looking for my company," said the frightened Jerseyman.

"Company, dang it! Form on the colors or you'll have no company. That's right, Shirtsleeves ; form on the colors." And then, as old Zeno appeared behind him, "Take these colors, darkey, and stand here till I bid you move." He ran down the extemporized platoon, and dressed it by pushing or pulling the men. "Load while we wait," he said to them in a loud tone, and then running back to the black man, "Form on the colors, boys, form on the colors!"

A minute was enough to bring in thirty or more men of every arm—dragoons without horses, artillerymen from Knox's brigade, riflemen of Morgan's, and infantry from half a dozen regiments. Well pleased, Elam now took the colors from Zeno, and gave them to a sixfooter from the Blue Ridge, saying :

"Bid them form on the colors, and as soon as you get forty men, find an officer, if you can. But, anyway, as soon as you have forty, follow me."

Then, running in front of his extemporized company:

"Mark time, gentlemen; poise firelocks, column of fours—forward, march—quick time."

And the little company disappeared into the darkness, while the Virginian in his turn shouted:

"Form on the colors. Why don't you form on the colors?"

A minute more, and Elam had his men on the run in double-quick time. Just in time was he to post them behind the wreck of a fence, built above some prostrate logs where the old road made a sharp bend northward, and where they had thus much cover as they lay, which in the darkness might deceive the advancing cavalry. He was just in time. Not one minute passed before the Englishmen came down the road in fours.

"Hold your fire till I bid," said Elam. "Remember Bunker's Hill, every baby of you. Hold your fire. I tell you I was there. Butternut, Shirtsleeves, Number Two, Peleg, cover your men when they pass the tree, and fire when you have them. That will do."

Crack! crack! crack! crack! These were the answers to the order, and the poor doomed fellows rolled off their horses, every man of them. The whole advancing column reined up in wild confusion.

"Storrow's company to the right! Double-quick time!" cried Elam. "Three files to the bridge! Double-quick time! Curtis, send to the general that we have every man of them."

Whether these impromptu commands to imagined forces were heard or not, it would be hard to say. The unfortunate commander of the English party was killed. His most experienced captain was at that moment feeling his way with a broken arm around the inner walls of Elam's cellar, two miles away. The other captain in the rear was giving orders, which no man heard in the wild confusion. A storm of random pistol shots from excited troopers confused everything, and made order impossible. All of them had for five minutes heard the drums of Faunce's company behind them, and from the way his boys beat them, you would have thought there were forty drums. They dared not, therefore, turn upon their own tracks, to meet a regiment of infantry in their rear.

The rear files of the English horsemen thought, and thought wisely, that discretion was the better part of valor. They leaped the low fence on their right, ran their horses to the river, and crossed it on the ice. A moment more and the same movement became universal. Men who thought, thought it had been ordered. Men who did not think, followed because it promised safety. Sooner than he meant, sooner than he wished, Elam saw his enemy retiring.

"Give them a volley, boys! Fire!" he cried, almost disappointed. And the men fired, probably with no effect. At that moment Light-horse Harry himself, with a squadron of some thirty men, appeared. Elam pointed eagerly to the flying foe.

Lee thanked him, and followed.

"Tally-ho, gentlemen!" he cried to his men, and they, too, leaped the fence in pursuit.

"Well, boys," said Elam, "Guess our job's done. Form on your sergeants. Column of fours. Quick-time—march."

At this moment Faunce and his men came up, well flushed with running, and well pleased with success.

They followed Elam's command. He led the whole party back to General Smallwood's headquarters. He met the tall Virginian with the second company.

"All out!" he called; "all out!" in the quaint phrase of the old-time fire companies. And this company also returned to the stable-yard of the old tavern, and, like Ford's men and Faunce's, stood at easy rest, listening to know if there were any other alarm.

No! the work was done, and well done. Smallwood himself and the gentlemen of his staff were sitting on their horses. From time to time one and another orderly or mounted officer rode in, and reported that all was still. A buzz and whisper, after half an hour, told that young Hamilton had ridden in with a message from the commander-in-chief. Smallwood himself now rode across to the improvised infantry.

"Captain," he said to Elam, "his Excellency is on the road, and will be here in a minute. Will you call your men into line that we may salute him?"

"Attention, company! Right dress! Poise firelocks! Shoulder firelocks! Slow time—march!" cried Elam.

"Attention, company! Right dress! Poise firelocks! Shoulder firelocks! Slow time—march!" cried the tall Virginian.

And Faunce repeated the order.

The clatter of horses' hoofs and the well-appointed staff of the commander-in-chief rode up. Washington himself was at Smallwood's side, and gave him his hand in eager congratulation.

"Present arms! Present arms!"

Washington turned to the men, uncovered his head, and said:

"We cannot thank you enough, gentlemen! With such soldiers America will never be conquered. A merry Christmas to you all!"

Then he bent in the saddle, took Elam Ford by the hand, and said:

"The best parade I ever saw, sir! May I know your rank and name?"

"Elam Ford, private, Massachusetts 19th, under arrest," said Elam, proud as Cœur de Lion.

"I am obliged to you none the less, captain," said Washington, pressing his hand this time. "We shall know each other better. You may dismiss your men. The alarm is over. A merry Christmas, boys!"

"General," said Smallwood, "if you would dismount, there is a cold turkey here and a glass of good Madeira. Ask your gentlemen to join us. Colonel Lee will be thirsty after his long ride, and we shall all wait for him." Then turning to Ford and beckoning to Faunce and to the Virginian, "Gentlemen, will you also join us in a glass of wine?"

He whispered to his orderly, and in a minute more the bugler, who had just now blew so different a strain, was sounding forth to the wind:

"Pease upon a trencher—pease upon a trencher."

The extemporized party was scarcely as noisy as that whose places they had taken.

The start which they all had was too fresh, and all ears were too much on the alert for a new alarm.

Washington was courteous; Hamilton was affable; Reed made himself at home; and Smallwood, trying to put all his guests at ease, called Lafayette, who had returned with the commander-in-chief.

"Marquis, if you ever want to teach the king's infantry of the line how to rally in a panic, ask this gentleman to give you lessons. By Jove, I sat my horse in wonder to see those frightened boys fall in."

And he presented Ford to the marquis, and they took wine together.

A minute more, and with a little bustle, Glover and Larned and Patterson came in.

"We have come to finish the Madeira, general," said Patterson, laughing.

"Then my bugler blew loud enough to call you?"

"We heard him as we came. To tell the truth, Glover was not unwilling." And they could all afford to laugh now.

Then they also saw the commander-in-chief, and apologized to him, and exchanged their formal congratulations.

"Glover," said Smallwood, who did not mean to forget his new friend, Elam Ford, "you Yankees do not know much about Christmas."

"We know good Madeira when we see it," said Glover, laughing.

"They do say you Marblehead men steer your regiments with a tiller and a rudder," said Smallwood, and the laugh was turned again. "I won't say much for your general; but for me, if I am to turn out in two minutes in the dark again, I hope I may have a private of the 19th to rally my men under fire."

For the first time, Glover took in the position. But he was quick, and though he did not know Elam Ford by sight, he understood it. He bowed, well pleased at the compliment to his men.

"I always told you that I had not a man in my brigade but what would make a good colonel."

"Well said, general," said Washington, smiling, "and very true. Will you oblige general and gentlemen by drinking the health of Captain Elam Ford? To our better acquaintance, Captain Ford.

"Really, Smallwood, I must not stay another minute.

"We thought we would look at all the forts. If we find any other company paraded, we shall want to wish them a merry Christmas."

PROMOTION.

At brigade general headquarters of "Glover's," on the 27th of December, the whole brigade paraded. At the end of the parade the officer on duty read the general order, which closed with the words:

"For gallantry in action, Private Elam Ford is relieved from arrest.

"For gallantry in action, at the special request of his Excellency the Commander-in-chief, Private Elam Ford is promoted to serve as captain, vice Wilderspin transferred to the naval service."

As Mr. Menet ended, a stalwart old lumberman, in the back of the car, rose and said through his nose, quite loud:

"I should like to have the privilege to enquire, be that story true?"

"Well," said Menet, laughing, "I tell it as I found it."

"I went over the ground once," said the professor, "with the story in my hand. It might have happened—it might have happened."

"A good many things mought have happened," said the lumberman.

And the others assented.

CHAPTER VIII.

HEPZIBAH'S TURKEYS.

HECTOR called again, in a broad grin :
"Four. Mrs. Fréchette will make a confession."
Mrs. Fréchette sprang to her feet at once.
"In sack-cloth and ashes I confess that Mr. Van Sandfoord is a humbug and cheat. I introduced him to his place, I made him chairman of the committee. I confess I was a fool. I confess that he was quite incapable from the beginning—"
And we were all in a shout of laughter, when poor Hector, a little upset, it must be confessed, turned to his sheet, and had to read :
"Fifth. Mrs. Van Sandfoord will tell the story of her life."
"My life has been so long," said the pretty little bride, blushing, "that you will not care to hear the whole of it.
"But while Mr. Decker read us his Thanksgiving story, I remembered one experience one day, which I saw in the life of one of my companions in Sunday-school.
"When my life is edited, this can come in as an episode in the sixteenth chapter of my eighteenth year.
"And our friend will be pleased to know that this story is true.
"I have it here written out in my scrap-book. It is called here

"HEPZIBAH'S TURKEYS."

INTRODUCTORY.

It is all sixteen years ago. Had the lives of the turkeys been spared, as they were not, they would all now be sweet seventeen. They might have rivalled in size the sixty-pound turkeys which Josselyn saw here two hundred years ago.*

But their lives were not spared.

The first I heard of the turkeys was as I came down from the pulpit on the Sunday morning before Thanksgiving. Miss Maria Jennings had worked her way to the neighborhood of the pulpit stairs, and beckoned me. I joined her.

"I wanted to ask you if you remember Hepzibah Brown?"

"Of course I do," said I—"the girl with the blind mother."

"The same," said Miss Maria. "You know she is in my Bible-class. I had thought that it would be a nice thing to suggest to the other girls, who have not the slightest idea what hardship is (as how should they?), to suggest to them that we would surprise Hepsie and her mother with a Thanksgiving dinner. Poor souls, I do not know how else they should have one. You do not see any harm, do you?"

"Harm? Not the least," said I; "but a great deal of good, rather."

"She will not be offended or hurt, will she?"

"I never saw that she was a fool," said I. "If she is, we had better all of us find it out. I should say,

---

* "I have heard several credible persons affirm they have seen turkie-cocks that have weighed forty, yea, sixty pound."—Josselyn's "Wonders," *Archæologia Americana*, vol. 4, p. 144.

hough, that 'never anything can be amiss when simileness and duty tender it.'"

Miss Maria laughed and went her way ; and, when he Bible-class gathered, she proposed her little plan to hose of the girls who came in before Hepzibah Brown lid, and bade them propose it to those who came in fter her. They were all pleased with the proposal, nd, as Monday and Tuesday passed, they brought ound to Miss Maria more money for their contribuions to the turkey than she really knew well what to lo with. I met her Wednesday morning, and she told ne so. But she said she had bought her turkey, and iad ordered home with him squashes and apples and cranberries and a bag of flour. Then, as cranberries vere useless without sugar and pies profitless without :heese, she had added twenty pounds of sugar and ive of cheese. She had a little money left, and she vas going to send a few pounds of tea to the old lady.

THE TURKEYS ARRIVE.

Hepzibah Brown was most briefly described, as the eader has seen, "as the girl who had the blind nother." Her mother had lost her sight long, long before I knew anything about either of them ; nor do know how she lost it. I first found them living in wo rooms, of which Hepzibah had to pay the rent veekly, and for which she provided the ways and neans by the most difficult and trying works and days. She went out to "days' works," technically so called. She occasionally contracted to take in babies by the nonth, in which case she invariably spent on their nilk much more than all the money paid to her ; and n a sharp strain she took in slop-work to sew upon.

But we all knew that times were indeed hard when she came to this resource.

For her mother there were several sources of revenue, which required nursing and tending worthy of Huskisson or Vansittart. There was the monthly payment of one dollar and sixty-two cents to each of the descendants of Jairus Hotchkiss. You had to go for this money at quarter before eleven on the second Friday before the third Thursday in the month. "It would derange my accounts," said the lady treasurer, "if they came at any other time." Then there was a dollar and a half a month from the Widows' Association. This you went for in the afternoon of the first Saturday in the month. It was steady pay; but it made it necessary for the old lady to stay in Boston through all the summer, for fear she would lose her "residence." Indeed, Hepzibah had once or twice been tempted to take lodgings in Dorchester, where rents were much lower; but she had resisted the temptation, because in that case she (or her mother, strictly) would have been cut off the list of the Association. For the Association saw some advantages which I do not see in keeping such people cooped up together in the town. The Overseers of the Poor of Boston have similar rules. The old lady drew two dollars a month from them; and she was right careful to go for that dole regularly, and not to slip into any bosky dells, to which it would not follow her. I think her husband had been a pump and block maker; and the "Seamen's Society," seeing that by virtue of the pumps he dealt in water and by virtue of the blocks was conversant with running rigging, took him on their lists, with a loyal indifference to red-tape, for which I blessed them.

That brought in a dollar and a quarter a month more.

Did I hear you grumbling, my dear Tyrus, because the Golconda and Crœsusberg divided only five and a half per cent in September, while you had had six per cent every six months before since you can remember?

Please spend half an hour, then, with a bit of paper, arranging your monthly personal expenses on such a scale of Debit that a little balance will be left to you when you have added up these four Credits:

Cr.

City of Boston,	$2.00
Jair. Hotchk.,	1.62½
Widows' Association,	1.50
Pump and Block,	1.25

I ask you to make out this little monthly statement of expenses—including your share of two dollars a week rent—because the calculation of these figures, arranged in different ways, took up most of the waking hours of Hepzibah Brown, when she lay awake at all.

For Hepzibah Brown herself, she tried hard not to beg, and liked to avail herself of the public means of culture and enjoyment. She was much more cheaply dressed than any of the other girls in Miss Maria's Bible-class. But she loyally came to the Bible-class, and I honored her for it, and so did Miss Maria. She sometimes indulged herself in tickets to a course of Lowell lectures on the "Non-metallic Bodies" or the "Correlation of Forces." She could get the tickets by standing in the street in a queue of half a mile, on her way home from Jairus Hotchkiss's. And in the evening, at the lectures, she saw the people. As she said herself, it saved gas and coal from seven o'clock till nine. It was true that the old lady could not see the experiments or the other illustrations. But she liked society, was glad to be in a crowd; and, as Hepzibah truly said, it was hard to get her out, and this was a good excuse for a walk for her.

They kept up, I think, between themselves, at most times, the pretence of much more ease of circumstance than ever existed or had existed. Sometimes there had to be some such frank exhibit as I have made above. But in general both of them thought something was going to turn up. They had, as all cheerful people have, great facility at discounting all their anticipations. And it was only when some lady visitor of the Hotchkiss charity, or some committee on retrenchment of the "Association" forced Hepzibah to state the narrowness of her circumstances that she herself was really aware quite how hard her case was. She would, as I said, add up her mother's income in many different ways; but the result in all was substantially the same. Still, by casting it upon the basis of a year it seemed a good deal more than when she did it monthly. And she, therefore, sometimes indulged herself in observing that it was seventy-six dollars and fifty-one cents a year, and that was a great deal of money; and that with seventy-six dollars and fifty-one cents a great deal can be done. In general, they affected, even with each other, to be well satisfied with the outlook, and sure that the present hard times would soon be over, and things in general easier to everybody.

In this mood, on the Wednesday after Miss Maria made the move about the turkeys in the Bible-class, Hepzibah said, as she poured out her second cup of tea, as she and her mother lingered at breakfast:

"I don't mean to take much trouble about Thanksgiving this year. The last time I roasted a turkey it took a heap of wood and made me no end of trouble. I was glad o' the trouble, 'cause I knew poor Jethro 'd have no turkey anywhere else. And he did take pleasure in that turkey, anyway. But Jethro (well, I s'pose Jethro must be in the Sandwich Islands, mother, now), he won't be here. And Sally told me she should be out to Melrose. There won't be nobody but you and me, and I don't think it's worth while bothering about the turkey. I've got to go at one to help 'em at Miss Scarlett's. They'll have a heap of people to-morrow, and I told Miss Scarlett 't, if I could, I'd come round. It would be a plague to you to be fussing over the gravy, if we had the turkey; so I guess we won't have none. When I get home from Miss Scarlett's I'll just roll out a little paste, and I can mix up and kind o' stew a few cran'bries 'fore I go to bed; and if you'd stone some raisins, as you sit here to-day, I'll mix a little plum pudding to-morrow, and we'll call that our Thanksgiving."

The old lady expressed her entire satisfaction, said she should eat no turkey herself, if they had any; that she thought it would be as much bother to her as it would be to Hepzibah. And they thus disguised from each other the truth, which was perfectly well known to both of them, that a turkey for Thanksgiving was as unattainable as was Aladdin's roc or a roc's egg, had they taken any fancy that way.

At noon the two took another cup of tea together and each ate a cold sausage. Hepzibah said she was rather in a hurry to get round to Miss Scarlett's, because they would not be able to do nothing till she got there, and would be kinder expecting her. She would not get a regular dinner, therefore, at home, unless her mother particularly wished it. Her mother replied that she did not feel much like eating, and had thought of suggesting that they should not set the table for dinner, but have a bit of bread and butter and a cup of tea. So they were both satisfied, or pretended to be, and Hepzibah went to Miss Scarlett's.

She had not been gone more than half an hour when the old lady, sitting in that eternal darkness, was roused from her after-luncheon doze by a rap at the door. She cried, "Come in!" as loudly as her weak old voice would say so; and Miss Maria entered, cheerily and cordially. She was no stranger in the place, and Mrs. Brown recognized her knock, step, and voice immediately. Miss Maria was a little disappointed that she did not find Hepzibah; but was glad to find she had "got work." She inquired carefully about Mrs. Brown's health; and, which was much more to the point, listened faithfully and patiently to the old lady's answer—a thing philanthropists are not quite so sure to do as they are to make the proper inquiries. Miss Maria then said she thought times were going to mend, and that it would be a mild winter, and that work would be more plenty than ever, and that she thought Hepzibah would have more than she could do; for which opinions I am afraid Miss Maria was largely indebted to a cheerful temper. Still, as she held them, in a certain form, I am glad that she expressed them to poor old Mrs. Brown, who certainly needed all the comfort she could pick up, and whose means of knowing the "mind of the street" on such subjects were limited. Then Miss Maria said she could not make a long call, and came to the proper object of her visit.

She went to the door, and, with her own red right hand, brought in the turkey, which she had waiting there for a surprise. Ah me! There was no need of leaving it outside to surprise old Mrs. Brown. Miss Maria might have brought in a feather-bed on her back, and the old lady would not have known it in that eternal midnight.

As it was, Miss Maria brought in her plump eleven-pounder, and put it on the table at the old lady's side, and explained that the young ladies at the Bible-class had arranged the dinner, as a surprise for Hepzibah, and made as if she had herself nothing to do with the affair. Then she tapped at the window, and Phineas came up-stairs from the doorway, where he had been waiting for the proper moment in the surprise, with the sugar and tea and cranberries and squashes, the cheese and apples, and the bag of flour. She explained what these "fixin's" were, and was about to leave somewhat abruptly, when the old lady, who was really very thankful and behaved very sweetly through the whole, asked her if Phineas would mind putting all the things into the store-closet, and laying the turkey on a certain shelf which she described, high above the highest flight of the cat in the back entry. For, she said, it occurred to her that it would be very good fun to surprise Hepzibah when she came back from Miss Scarlett's. I ought perhaps to mention, in this place, that it was now forty years since " Miss" Scarlett had been united in marriage to the Hon. Le Fevre Scarlett—she having been Miss Lilian White—and that the title " Miss" was merely the form used by the aborigines in describing the condition of honorable wedlock.

Phineas gladly fell in with all Mrs. Brown's devices, and the stores were concealed, according to her order. She had relapsed into stoning the raisins, after knitting a few rounds on a long stocking, which " Miss" Plumptre had sent the yarn for, and which was to be sent to a Maori chieftain when it was finished and when its companion was finished, when she was aroused again by the sharp closing of the outer door down-stairs. There was no room for question as to the step on the stairs this time. Men and angels knew that step as the step of Officer Fosdick, who was this week on the day patrol in Lucas Street ; and Mrs. Brown, who was neither a man nor an angel, knew it as well as if she had been both at once. Hastily she ran through the little catalogue of her sins and Hepzibah's, inquiring which of them fell within the category of crimes prohibited by the law. She was certain that they had not thrown marbles at an auctioneer, as Harry Griggs did, and was sent to Westborough for doing it. Certainly they had not lifted ribbons from Mudge's, as that odious Miss Farrelly did, in the next house, when the neighborhood was disgraced by her arrest. She knew that the pipes and faucets had not been protected against the cold ; but she did not believe that there yet had been any frost hard enough to catch them, and she and Hepsie were, as usual, running for luck, in the hope that there might not be. As Officer Fosdick stumped up the stairs Mrs. Brown thus exhausted her catalogue of crime, and with conscious innocence uttered a severe " Come in !"

" How do, Miss Smith ?" said Officer Fosdick, civilly enough. " Thanky mum, I'm pretty well myself. Isn't your daughter to home ?"

" No, sir," said Mrs. Brown, still with conscious innocence and greatly aggrieved. " Hepzibah is not at home." Was she to rejoice or not at her absence ? Suppose Hepzibah were to be arrested at some distance from home, what would become of Mrs. Brown ?

" Sorry, mum," said Officer Fosdick ; " but it's just

as well, seeing you are." Horrible suspense to Mrs. Brown! Suppose she were arrested and haled to prison, as Paul and Silas were at Philippi, what would happen when Hepzibah returned?

But the suspense did not last many seconds. Officer Fosdick continued, in a tone which showed that he was well pleased:

"The captain sends his compliments, mum, to you and your daughter, mum; and here's a turkey, mum, for Thanksgiving. There's been a little subscription at the station, mum, to give turkeys to them as might not—well, as might not have thought to buy 'em, mum, and the captain said himself, mum, that he wanted to be sure you had one, mum."

It was well that the officer's speech was long, for Mrs. Brown thought, at the beginning, that he was announcing the same turkey which Miss Jennings had brought. But she recovered herself, without betraying the fact that another turkey had arrived, which might have mortified him. She thanked him very courteously, and then, at his request, "hefted" the turkey; the only way by which she could judge what a "noble crittur it was." She then asked him if he would be so kind as to put it into the closet, which she pointed out to him, next the stove.

Officer Fosdick did so. If he were a little surprised at seeing the squashes and parcels which Phineas had left there, he said nothing. "I've hung her up, mum, on a nail they is in the top shelf, mum," said he. And Mrs. Brown thanked him, and he bade farewell.

She fell back upon her knitting and upon planning out the devices by which she would make of the two turkeys a surprise to Hepzibah when she returned. But she had not knit twenty times round when she heard the outer door open and shut again. Nobody ever rings at these lodging-houses; indeed, the bell-wires were long since broken at all of them. The step this time was wholly unknown to Mrs. Brown. But the stranger did not pass the door, but knocked loudly.

"Come in."

"Do Mrs. and Miss Brown live here?" said the gray-coated coachman, whip in hand, who entered.

"I am Mrs. Brown. My daughter is not at home."

"Just as well, ma'am," and the man disappeared. But it was to return in a moment. "Mrs. Cradock sends her compliments, and hopes Mrs. Brown and Miss Brown will have a pleasant Thanksgiving. And Mrs. Cradock sends a turkey and a few other things. Where shall I leave them, ma'am?"

"Oh, just put them on the table. Thank you kindly. And tell Mrs. Cradock that we are very much obliged, I am sure. I hope she's very well."

"Thank you, ma'am, she's very well. Good-by, ma'am. I can't leave my horses." And the gray coachman, who to Mrs. Brown was no more gray than green, disappeared.

"Well, now," said she, as she crossed and "hefted" turkey No. 3, and smelled at the heavy package of Bohea, and did the same by the two squash pies that the man had left—"well, now, how shall I keep these out of Hepzibah's sight?" Carefully and successfully she opened a crypt under the sink, moved the pots all to one end, hung the turkey on a nail she remembered there, and then one by one she placed the other bounties in the store-closet, as she might.

A good deal flustered, she returned to her chair, to find that there were but three needles in her stocking.

This was a serious matter. And Mrs. Brown was on her knees on the floor, groping for the fourth needle, when she heard another rat-tat-tat at the door. She hurried to her feet as soon as she could and gave permission to enter.

It was Hitty. Hitty was wholly out of breath. "Miss Brown, I was standing up to the head of the court, and a lady come by, and asked if I knew where Miss Hepzibah Brown lived. And I said it was No. 7, up the street, up one flight. And she says, says she, 'I'm a little late for my car,' says she—just so. 'Will you just carry this turkey to Miss Hepzibah Brown, with my love?' And then she stopped; says she, 'It's Miss Brown that has a blind mother.' And I said, yes, Miss Hepsy Brown had a blind mother. And she gin me ten cents for bringing it, and here it is."

"Why, Hitty," said the old lady, amazed, "who was the lady?"

"Don't know," said Hitty. "I asked her, says I, 'Who shall I say it is?' says I. And she says, says she, 'Oh, she'll know,' says she. So she called the Norfolk House car, that was passing; and she got in, she did; and I come up here with the turkey, and here it is. It's real heavy, Miss Brown, and it's a beauty. I wish you could see it, Miss Brown. But do just heft it."

So Mrs. Brown "hefted" the turkey, as she had hefted three others.

"And now, Hitty, will you help me look for my knitting-needle. I was on the floor looking for it."

"It's pretty dark this side of the room, Miss Brown. Might I light a lamp?"

Poor Mrs. Brown! It was as light to her as it was

by the window. Hitty lighted her lamp, and went on her knees for the exploration. Rising, a little exhausted by the bending, she cried out, "Here it is, Miss Brown."

"Where was it, my dear child?"

"Oh, jest behind you, mum. Good-by."

Hitty's grammar was imperfect; but she had native politeness enough not to tell the old lady that the lost needle was stuck in her back hair. Unless some one reads to her this story, she will never know where that needle was till she dies.

She took the needle and worked faithfully on upon the Maori chieftain's stocking. Whether more turkeys would arrive she wondered. Whether she would secrete number four, or leave it where Hitty laid it. Finally she hung it on a nail behind the door by which Hepzibah would enter. So she knitted and dozed, and dozed and knitted. When the somewhat shaky clock which we then had on our church-tower struck seven, she laid down the Maori's garment, filled the teapot, put it on the stove, and filled up with kindling and wood. To say true, Mrs. Brown had wrapped her shawl tight round her as the afternoon passed, but had made no more fire than Hepzibah had left. She knew that Hepzibah might leave "Miss Scarlett's" as early as seven.

But it was eight and after before Hepzibah came. The tea-kettle had boiled long before (or the water in it), and had been set back to the rear of the stove, for a decorous simmer there. At last the well-known step sounded on the stair, and the hard-worked, long-waited-for absentee returned. She slyly laid down in the sink something heavy which she had in her hand, and came to her mother and kissed her; a token wholly unusual and unexpected in that establishment, in which no sentiment was ever wasted.

"What do you think, mammy, dear? I've changed my mind, and we will have a Thanksgiving dinner, after all."

"How did she know?" This was Mrs. Brown's only thought.

"You see, we had to fly round at Miss Scarlett's, I tell you. They're going to have all his brothers, and her sisters, and two judges from England, and I dunno what all, to dinner—goin' to set the table cornerwise in the big parlor of all ; and then they have a late tea and supper together, and have all the cousins 'way from West Newton and Brahntry—seventy-four in all. Jane Scarlett says to me, says she, 'Ther'll be seventy-four in all, if the weather's fine ; so Miss Byfield ken bring in her twins,' says she. And their famous Mrs. Midge, the grand cook, that they spoke for three months ago—she that makes their Marlboroughs and their open-top apple-pies—she hadn't come nigh 'em when I got there ; and Miss Scarlett and Jane Scarlett had to take hold themselves, and I had to spring to, I tell you ; and we have had a smart time of it since I was here. Well, I had my tea there ; and just as I come away Miss Scarlett, says she, 'Hepsy,' says she, 'you let John go home with you,' says she, 'and let him carry this turkey,' says she, 'for your mother,' says she ; 'for,' says she, 'your mother won't feel like going out to-morrow, Hepsy,' says she, 'and so,' says she, 'she better have her turkey to home, Hepsy,' says she. 'She did,' says she. So here's your turkey, mammy. He's a beauty. Do just heft him."

And Mrs. Brown hefted the fifth turkey. She was a little grieved to find the wind, in a measure, taken out of her sails ; but she concealed her grief, and in the darkness Hepzibah did not observe her expression. While she was busying herself in replenishing the fire, Mrs. Brown crossed the room and lifted down No. 4, so that he lay by the side of No. 5. Then, as Hepsy rose from her puffing and blowing, and lighted the lamp, she saw in a moment that there were twins where she had laid but one turkey ; and then the old lady was well satisfied with her amazement.

It is easy to imagine how she went on—how, when Hepsy opened the closet, to find No. 2, and the stores which surrounded him, the good old soul had one triumph more ; how then, by clumsy artifices, she made her look under the sink for No. 3 ; and at last fairly sent her into the back entry to see No. 1 upon his supra-feline shelf. A jolly evening had Mrs. Brown and Hepzibah with their jorums of tea from Miss Maria's paper and with the successive surprises.

They had both got to bed, and the light was blown out, when the outer door swung open again, and one more tramp was to be heard on the stairway.

"Gracious, mercy ! More turkeys !" cried Mrs. Brown.

" No," groaned Hepsy, " it is not turkeys this time. It's that drunken MacDonnell thundering up to beat his wife again."

Drunk or sober, the thunderer stopped at Hepsy's door and knocked.

" Who's there ?"

" Adams's Express. Parcel to be left to-night. Marked ' *without fail*,' " replied the thunderer, more good-naturedly than was to be expected.

Hepsy was striking a match. She arranged some

hurried and superficial toilet, and in a couple of minutes opened a crack of the door.

"You must give me more room, mum, or I can't get him in," said the good-natured thunderer.

"*Him?* Who is he?"

But as Hepsy opened the door wider, he appeared. The largest turkey of all, with his wings not clipped off.

"Orders are strict to be delivered to-night. Train late, mum—hopped a frog at Wilmington Junction. Guess the turkey's for Thanksgiving."

This last with a broad grin, as if the purpose might be questionable.

Sure enough, to Hepzibah's wondering eyes there appeared a large label: "To Miss Hepzibah Brown, No. 7 Lucas Street, second floor, with the respects of Ezekiel Hopkins. To be delivered this evening, WITHOUT FAIL." The gigantic letters at the close were enough to have alarmed or, at least, excited any reasonable expressman; nor had they failed.

Now, Ezekiel Hopkins was a tinman from Ipswich, who had been on the steamer "Creole" when Hepsy and her mother joined in the Foresters' excursion in the harbor, in September.

"Please receipt, mum," said the well-satisfied thunderer. And with trembling hand Hepzibah signed the receipt in his book. She bade the thunderer 'good-night and retired this time to unbroken slumbers.

Yes, Mathilde, to slumbers. She had had a turkey sent her from Ezekiel Hopkins. But she had scoured floors all the morning and worked loyally at the Scarlett's till near eight in the evening, and so she slept soundly, and would have done so had Ezekiel Hopkins sent three turkeys.

I am ashamed to confess that, when, the next Sunday, Hepzibah Brown gave me the heads of this story, briefly, as we left the church together, I was carnal enough to say:

"Well, I suppose Silas Brackett was glad to take off your hands all the turkeys you could not use."

Now, Silas Brackett kept the "provision store," as we Yankees call a small meat market, at the corner.

"I dare say," said Hepzibah, as proudly as Juno; "but he had no turkeys of mine to sell."

And I was thoroughly shamed when she added:

"I knew plenty of *poor* people that had no Thanksgiving dinner."

The emphasis on *poor* was superb. For once, Hepsy had had the satisfaction of dispensing charity; and no Mrs. Cradock, or Officer Fosdick, or Maria Jennings of them all would discharge that office more grandly nor more kindly than she.

She told me nothing about it; but there was little which passed in Lucas Street, or Carney Place, or Orange Lane in those days, which was not reported before the week was over to one or other of the saints who were at work in our sewing-room, and without much difficulty I was able to patch out the story I now tell to you.

Hepsy and her mother slept late on Thanksgiving morning. There was no "day's work" to be grateful for, at which one must report at seven o'clock, breakfast already eaten. Hepsy took the good of her bed, for once, and then made a fire lavishly. She had a week's provant in the house, and that was a very long forelook for her. A sumptuous breakfast she and Mrs.

Brown made; and then Hepsy assumed the Lady Bountiful, as if she had been born to the position.

"I hate to leave you, mother; but it's Thanksgiving day, and I think, before meeting, I'll just step round into Orange Lane, and see how those poor Flannagans get on. I hadn't any time to go and see them yesterday. We sha'n't want to put our turkey in the oven before eleven. I'll just stuff him and get him ready now, and then I'll be back in time to put him in. Perhaps you would not mind pounding the cracker."

All this without the slightest allusion to the theory of yesterday morning's breakfast, that the roasting of the turkey would be a useless bother.

So they quickly got the great fowl ready, and then Hepsy arrayed herself in her Sunday's best for her visit to the Flannagans. Ah me! That was what the philanthropists are apt to say is " not a good case." Indeed, it was not a good case. Hepsy went in cordially, but with a consciousness of her dignity and position, and of the distinction which must be preserved between the classes of society. Mrs. Flannagan, careworn and wretched, welcomed her and wiped the seat of the only chair with her apron. Hepsy inquired by name after the children, and then how Mike was doing. "How do you do?" means one thing, my dear Mrs. Whitehead or my dear Mrs. Lovechild, when Fanny comes running into your parlor, and says, "How do you do?" to you. But when you ask how Mike Flannagan is doing, the question means simply is he getting along without making a beast of himself or no. Alas! Mike was not doing well. He had assisted in a turkey raffle the night before to such purpose that he had spent all the money which they would advance him at Hinckley's, that he had won no turkey, and that he had been brought back at one in the morning by Britt and Flinders, who were only not quite so drunk as he was. Mrs. Flannagan pointed sadly into the dark alcove, on the straw on the bottom of which Mike was sleeping off his whiskey, much as a pig might sleep in the covered part of his stye.

"Too bad," said Hepsy. "Too bad, Mary. Hanging is not good enough for them that give him the liquor. But he's well at home now. I'll come round in the morning with Mac, and we'll make him take the pledge before he goes out. Don't you say a word to him to-day. I came 'round because I want Larry for an hour or two; and if you will let him come with me he shall bring you a nice turkey for your Thanksgiving dinner. So do you take heart, Mary, and you shall have a good, pleasant Thanksgiving, after all. You see my turkey raffle turned out better than Mike's."

Poor Mary would not laugh, but she gave her consent gladly enough to Larry's going with Hepsy, and Hepsy started in search of him among the boys who were skating on the frozen puddle behind the stables.

Larry, as need hardly be said, was immensely excited by the commission. He borrowed Hiram Flinders's four-wheel, when he found what was in the wind; went back with Hepsy to Lucas Street, took in his freight, and decorously accompanied her, with as much dignity as Mrs. Cradock's coachman would have shown on the morning's expedition. First they came back to his mother's; and Mrs. Flannagan had to take a regular talking to from Lady Bountiful as to how the turkey was to be stuffed and basted. Let us trust that she obeyed the injunctions. Then they went to little Mrs. Serz, in the cellar in Castle Street. Hepsy worked her way in with some difficulty, for the muslin skirt of Gertrude MacFlimsey hung across the room from one side to another, as it was drying. In the window corner Mrs. Serz was doing crimping, or fluting, or clear starching, or some deed without a name.

"Good-morning, Miss Serz."

"*Guten Morgen, guten Morgen.*"

"A nice day for Thanksgiving, Miss Serz."

"*Nicht verstehe, nicht verstehe.*"

"Glad to see you so well. But it's a shame you have to work on Thanksgiving."

"*Nicht verstehe, nicht verstehe.*"

"Thank you kindly, she's very well. We had a turkey we could not use, Mrs. Serz, and I thought you might like it."

Mrs. Serz was a little amazed by this time, and looked for Constance, who could interpret a little. But Hepsy was before her, and called in Larry.

"Here's the turkey, Miss Serz. And if you have got a little cracker, you can pound it with sweet marjoram. We think that makes better stuffing, in our country, than bread and onions do." This last she said very loud, from the fear that it might not be entirely intelligible.

Mrs. Serz looked with amazement at the turkey, wiped her hands and "hefted" him, and said:

"*Danke, danke.*"

"I say without onions. Onions are better with geese. But I put in this little paper of sweet marjoram. It is some I brought from Tuxbury." This last very loud, as Mrs. Serz seemed somewhat doubtful.

"*Danke, danke,*" said that lady again.

And Hepsy withdrew. Larry followed, crestfallen. Why did she say "Donkey," he asked Miss Hepsy, meekly. But Miss Hepsy returned no answer.

"Larry," said she, after a little consideration, "we must go next to Phil Regan's ; and then we will come back by Suffolk Street, to them Eyetallians."

To Phil Regan's attic they repaired, therefore. Phil was not at home. He was blacking shoes at the Albany Station. But Phil's smart little sister Florence was in, and the other two little ones. No school. So Hepsy took off her bonnet and shawl, mixed the cracker crumbs to suit herself, and explained carefully to Florence how she wished to have the turkey basted, and with her own hands put it into the pan and put the pan into the oven, giving Florence strict directions how to tend it and watch over it till Phil returned. Brave Phil Regan, the head of that household! I wonder where he is to-day, and whether he will read this. He was just then fourteen years old.

At the Eyetallians much such a scene transpired as at Mrs. Serz's, Hepsy being wholly ignorant of any dialect of the Tuscan tongue ; and the Eyetallians, who had come on from New York only ten days before, equally ignorant of English. But there was no misunderstanding Miss Hepsy's kindness of intention ; and as she spoke very loud here, it is to be hoped that the Eyetallians understood the greater part of her directions to them. Anyway, the two women, with many "*grazie*," took the turkey as gently as if it had been a baby, and Hepsy, in a thorough examination of the attic, well-nigh empty, was soon satisfied that no one had been before her there. Nay, she even wondered whether in the calendar of these poor Roman Catholics the name of "Thanksgiving" had ever come in before. But by mentioning it sufficiently loudly she felt sure that she should fix it in their minds.

As they went back toward Lucas Street, Larry

following behind, a carriage, driving fast, passed them.

"Miss Hepsy, Miss Hepsy!" cried Larry, out of breath. "Sure as I live, there's your mother goin' to ride."

"Nonsense, Larry. None of your stuff."

"I say, Miss Hepsy, it was your mother, sure as I live and breathe."

"Hold your tongue, Larry."

And he held it.

But when Hepsy had climbed the stairway to her own home, sure enough the bird had flown. Mrs. Brown was not there. Nobody was there.

Hepsy ran into the bedroom in a fright. No mother there. She came back to Larry, and questioned him. He was stanch in saying that the old lady was in the kerridge.

Hepsy returned amazed to the sitting-room which her mother had not left without her for five years and more.

As she entered it by one door, the door to the back passage opened also, and two fresh, pretty girls came out, one bearing Miss Maria's turkey in state, and the other following with a dredging-box and an armful of other cooking tools.

"O Hepsy, you have caught us. That's too bad!"

And they all laughed heartily.

It was Ruth Faxon and Fanny Melcher. They had come round with Mrs. Granger, resolved to make Mrs. Brown and Hepsy go off to meeting, while they cooked the turkey. Hepsy was to be free from care that day, if it could be managed.

"And now, you provoking old thing, you went and stayed out till the bell had done tolling, and you have spoiled all. But we dressed up your dear old mother, and Mrs. Granger has carried her away ; and don't you think, Hepsy, now, that you had better go, too, and tell us what the text is?"

"Fiddlestick for the text," said Hepsy, hanging up her go-to-meeting shawl and bonnet in her chamber, and coming out with her sleeves rolled up, as if she, too, were going into action.

"What do you mean by interfering with other people's work?" said Fanny ; and she took her fast by both arms and pushed her back into her mother's deep arm-chair.

"There, you provoking old thing, if you do mean to stay and spy on us, sit there, and see if we do not know how to do it right. You are a fine lady to-day, just recovering from a fit of neuralgia, and you have just stepped into your kitchen for a minute, to see if these two girls, that have just come down from Nova Scotia and want a place together, know beans or not. Oh dear! I have not had such a lark since we were all at the Winthrop together !"

The Winthrop, dear Matilda, was not a hotel, but a school, where these three girls had studied arithmetic, side by side, under Miss Barry's eye, when they were all fourteen years old.

And a genuine lark they had of it. Neatly and deftly these two girls prepared and baked the turkey, boiled the squash, baked the potatoes, thickened the gravy, sweetened the cranberry to Hepsy's taste, and, in short, made all things ready for the dinner. They asked her for her orders sometimes ; but when she herself undertook to do anything one or other of them pushed her back into the easy-chair. Ruth gave her a smelling-bottle, which she raked out from a deep pocket, and folded a New York *Ledger* into a great fan, and made her hold the fan in one hand and salts in the other. Hepsy entered into the joke as much as they did, and took airs admirably well.

By the time Mrs. Brown had come home, the dinner was cooked, the table was neatly set, and everything was ready.

"Hepsy," said the old lady, "come here." And she whispered to her daughter.

Hepsy laughed, and said openly to the girls that her mother was so much pleased with the festivity, that she wanted to bring out her silver spoons. And, sure enough, the six teaspoons and the six tablespoons were produced from the old lady's trunk—the one wreck from old prosperity.

"I do not choose to use them every day," said Hepsy, laughing, " we have such queer people round us. But to-day mammy feels grand."

And then the two girls went away, only feeling a little dashed, as pretty Ruth Faxon confessed to me, that they left the two all alone.

The minute they were gone, before dinner began, Hepsy dashed into the back entry and seized turkey No. 6, which Fanny had left all dressed and ready for the oven, put him in a pan, and slid it into the stove. "I'm not going to waste this good fire," said she. " And I like a cold turkey about as well as I do a warm one. This will do for Sunday's dinner."

The old lady said that, of the two, she was not sure but sometimes she liked a cold turkey better than a warm one. Just now she was glad they had a hot one. The opinion, you see, was rather a difficult one to form and to express. But Mrs. Brown had long experience in contentedness. Turkey No. 6 being well slid into the oven, dinner began.

But scarcely had Hepzibah begun her carving when steps were heard on the stairs, which indicated a party.

"I guess Miss Meldrum has company," said she.
No. It was not Miss Meldrum.
Knock at the door—double knock.
"Well, I never!" said the old lady. "'Nother turkey, Hepsy?"

For Mrs. Brown was up to joking-mark now. Hepsy opened the door.

"Well now!" "How *do* you do?" "And how do *you* do?" "Well! what luck!" "Who'd a thought it?" "And there's your mother." "How d'ye do, Aunt Rachel?" "But who is it?" "Well, now!" "Well, now!" Scatter these ejaculations as you please, and you get the interview. They were cousins of Hepzibah's, whom she had not seen for fifteen years. They were on their way from New York to Cape Elizabeth, to dine at Hepsy's uncle. Boat was delayed, and they had missed their train. Thought they would hunt up Hepsy and take their Thanksgiving dinner with her, and so go on in the night boat to Portland.

Not unprosperous cousins, you see. Cousins who had no idea that Hepsy and her mother were uncomfortably near the wall. Cousins for whom Hepsy had a certain respect, and she would have hated to have them know her scrapings and worries.

"And here they come in, Mr. Hale, as nice and neat as pins; and though I say it, who should not, Mr. Hale, we was just as nice as they was. Mother, she did look real nice, Mr. Hale; real handsome she looked, with her cap on. And the table was so pretty—with Miss Granger's flowers, and the silver, and all. I did not care who they were; my dinner was as good as theirs any day. So they washed themselves and fixed their hair, and sat down, all three of them, they did. And we had a nice time, I tell you."

Hepsy did not tell me one little incident of the dinner; but Mrs. Meldrum did.

As they were finishing Mrs. Cradock's pies, drinking their tea, and fooling with their nuts and raisins, little Katy Meldrum came in.

"Please, Miss Hepsy, mother says will you lend her a little tea?"

"Heart's grace, Katy. Of course, I will. Why, Katy, you look cold."

Katy whispered that they had nothing but a little kindling.

"No coal? Poor child! Cousin Hannah, excuse me."

And Hepsy went into the entry and carried up a hod of coal to the stricken widow up-stairs.

"Do you think," she said, as she came down, "they was all sitting round freezing, and Miss Meldrum just lighting some laths the boys had brought in from the new school-house. And they've nothing for their dinner but some bread and cheese that look as if it was cut last Sunday. Here, Tom, you come in. Come in, Katy."

And she opened her oven door, and with the tongs pulled out No. 6, and placed the pan on a stout paper in her clothes-basket.

"Tom, you take one end. Katy, you take one. Tell your mother I've been cooking her dinner for her, only I was a little belated by company. Katy, come down again. Here's plenty of squash pie and two or three pertaters left. To think," said Hepsy, as she sat down a little flustered—" to think of plenty and hunger being so close to each other. I thought Mr. Fosdick had taken the Meldrums some dinner."

And then the feast went on with the three cousins, as if this were all an every-day occurrence. They went to their graves with the idea that Hepsy was living on the fat of the land. And, if any one thing delighted Hepsy more than another in that day's Thanksgiving, it was that her cousins thought so.

Among them they brought Miss Maria's turkey near his end ; but Hepsy told me that he made a very good dinner on Friday.

It may add to the interest with which this little story is read for me to say that it is substantially true in all its details.

The Independent asked me near a year ago to furnish a story of true life from my ministerial experience. On such stories there is apt to be a seal of confidence. But I do not see that any of the parties whom, under fictitious names, I have mentioned here, has reason to be ashamed of his part in the day, always excepting Mike Flannagan.

I have lost the run of him ; but I trust that he has taken Father Mathew's medal and has reformed.

And so poor Mrs. Fréchette's turn came round again.

The pitiless Hector, a little recovered, so soon as

there had been a reasonable pause after his wife's story, turned, as if surprised, to the programme, and read :

"Six. Mrs. Fréchette will read an essay."

She was ready for him again. "I observe with pleasure," she said, "that nothing is said about the essay being original. I had proposed to read, therefore, Lord Bacon's 'Essay on Gardening,' which seems very appropriate here. But talking with Mr. Hackmatack at breakfast, I have found that he had with him a curious discussion by his friend, Mr. Ingham, which he has lent me, as a substitute for that paper. I would read it now, but my friend Cæsar tells me that the Christmas dinner is ready, to which all our friends present are invited."

Sure enough, it was two o'clock already. With a little crowding, the whole party of passengers collected in the dinner car, and the dinner went forward, really much as was proposed in Hector's rodomontade of the bill of fare.

And without, steady snow—snow—snow, quiet drift —drift—drift. Half the engine was buried now. A mountain was before it. The shovellers had given up a useless duty. One or two of them were in the plough. The rest clustered in the forward car or with us. For all for whom there was not room in the dinner car, Hector took care that one and another substantial dish should be sent forward from the table.

And the party sang, and laughed, and chatted, and ate, and drank at their little tables, till, in spite of them, the day began to darken. It was half-past four.

"One last song," cried Hector. "I will sing you a song of one of Mrs. Fréchette's Tory ancestors." And he sang the old version of the "British Genadiers."

> "Come, come, fill up your glasses,
>   And drink a health to those
>   Who carry caps and pouches
>   And wear their loopéd clothes ;
>   For be you Whig or Tory,
>   Or any mortal thing,
>   Be sure that you give glory
>   To George, our gracious King !"

"That's what they sang at your Uncle Tracy's, madam. I wish you would take one more glass of anise-seed."

And so they slowly walked forward one by one from the car.

"Stay a moment, please," said Paul Decker to Theodora Bourn, as she folded her napkin and stood, as the stream passed by her.

"Please sit down a moment. I want to explain to you what I meant about learned women, when we were talking of Mrs. Browning. My—you know—of course I should not say—well, my own mother—how I wish you knew my mother, you would like her so ; she is as learned a woman as Lady Jane Grey—she taught me all my Greek when I went to college—and she keeps up with everything—and she is—oh, she is so lovely."

"O Mr. Decker, I understood you, I am sure. We all know that nobody has too much learning. Poor I ought to, who never saw the inside of a school-house till I was sixteen."

"Worse things can happen than that, I am sure," said he eagerly. "What I was driving at, when I blundered so, was that I do think book people are apt to get lonely, perhaps a little bit selfish. My old mentor used to say 'self-culture' was for the devil. Well now, you don't know, I do not suppose women can. But I have known—well in camp I have known— plenty of men whose books spoiled them. They could not speak a good word to a greaser or a ranchero. The men hated them, and no wonder. Yet they did not mean to be bad."

"They could not bear each other's burdens."

"Just so, and so in the end they could not bear their own; or, rather, nobody would give them any to bear."

"I know," said Theodora, "I know. I have seen just such people. There was a man in Sacramento— but no matter for him. I so wish you had known my dear mother. She had—oh, she had everything on her shoulders—but really, Mr. Decker, if any living being came into the room where she was, she would lay down her book or lay down her work, and pretend she was doing nothing, till she could make sure you did not want her—that she could not sew for you, or write for you, or read to you, or comfort you. She did not know how to think of herself."

"And that is the secret of it all," he said, so eagerly.

"And when we come to that, it all comes so clear—"

And so they went on—strangers no longer now—with a boy's discoveries and now a girl's of the mysteries of life, revenging themselves for the loneliness of these months that had been grinding by, in the satisfaction —what is like it?—of finding some one who has gone through something of the same desolation—each eager to find if the other had known this joy or that sorrow, and each finding out, almost with wonder, that this experience or that of life, which had seemed peculiar and quite without precedent, was an experience which the other knew.

They had sat there talking for more than an hour, when they heard singing from the palace car, and Theodora started. "We are staying here quite too long."

But Paul Decker did not think so.

He almost lifted her across the snowy platform.

"You cannot be too careful here."

Mrs. Fréchette and Professor Wisner, after they found each other out, had come into loyal alliance.

Hector had fired at random his announcement of "Prayer from Moses in Egypt." It seemed well enough for wanderers in a desert, and that was all he had thought of. But Mrs. Fréchette knew the music —indeed, the professor had the opera in print in his trunk—and while the others slept, or pretended to, after dinner, he had rallied an efficient quartette in the baggage car, so that when the indomitable Hector called to order, Dr. Wisner interrupted him to say:

"We propose here and now to introduce the celebrated prayer from Moses, which is the seventh number on the programme." And they so sang that magnificent chorus, that again every man and woman felt that the form of the celebration was not leading them from the genuine trust of Christmas day.

Van Sandfoord himself thanked them in the name of the assembly, most seriously and courteously, and then said, without banter now, "I think we are promised an essay by Mr. Hackmatack."

"Hardly," said George, "though the paper describes an essay or enterprise or experiment in my life. In truth, I did not write it. But it may be relied on, as if I had written it. It was all written out by a friend of mine, and Dr. Wisner is so kind as to read it as he put it down."

So Professor Wisner read the story of

IDEALS.

I. IN ACCOUNT.

I have a little circle of friends, among all my other friends quite distinct, though of them. They are four men and four women; the husbands more in love with their wives than on the days when they married them, and the wives with their husbands. These people live for the good of the world, to a fair extent, but much, very much, of their lives is passed together. Perhaps the happiest period they ever knew was when, in different subordinate capacities, they were all on the staff of the same magazine. Then they met daily at the office, lunched together perforce, and could make arrangements for the evening.

But, to say true, things differ little with them now, though that magazine long since took wings and went to a better world.

Their names are Felix and Fausta Carter, Frederic and Mary Ingham, George and Anna Haliburton, George and Julia Hackmatack.

I get the children's names wrong to their faces—except that in general their name is Legion, for they are many—so I will not attempt them here.

These people live in very different houses, with very different "advantages," as the world says. Haliburton has grown very rich in the rag and paper business, rich enough to discard rag money and believe in gold. He even spits at silver, which I am glad to get when I can. Frederic Ingham will never be rich. His regular income consists in his half-pay as a retired brevet officer in the patriot service of Garibaldi of the year 1859. For the rest, he invested his money in the Brick Moon, and, as I need hardly add, insured his life in the late Continental Insurance Company. But the Inghams find just as much in life as do the Haliburtons, and Anna Haliburton consults Polly Ingham about the shade of a flounce, just as readily and as eagerly as Polly consults her about the children's dentistry. They are all very fond of each other.

They get a great deal out of life, these eight, partly because they are so closely allied together. Just two whist parties, you see ; or, if they go to ride, they just fill two carriages. Eight is such a good number—makes such a nice dinner party. Perhaps they see a little too much of each other. That we shall never know.

They got a great deal out of life, and yet they were not satisfied. They found that out very queerly. They have not many standards. Ingham does take the *Spectator ;* Hackmatack condescends to read the *Times ;* Haliburton, who used to be in the insurance business, and keeps his old extravagant habits, reads both the *Advertiser* and the *Transcript ;* all of them have the *Christian Union*, and all of them buy *Harper's Weekly*. Every separate week of their lives they buy of the boys, instead of subscribing ; they think they may not want the next number, but they always do. Not one of them has read the *Nation* for five years, for they like to keep good-natured. In fact, they do not take much stock in the general organs of opinion, and the only standard books you find about are scandalously few. The Bible, Shakespeare, John Milton; Polly has Dante ; Julia has " Barclay's Apology," with ever so many marks in it ; one George has " Owen Felltham," and the other is strong on Marcus Aurelius.

Well, no matter about these separate things ; the uniform books besides those I named, in different editions, but in every house, are the "Arabian Nights" and "ROBINSON CRUSOE." Hackmatack has the priceless first edition. Haliburton has Grandville's (the English Grandville). Ingham has a proof copy of the Stothard. Carter has a good copy of the Cruikshank.

If you ask me which of these four I should like best, I should say, as the American Laureate did when they gave him his choice of two kinds of cake :

"Both's as good as one."

Well, "Robinson Crusoe" being their lay gospel and creed, not to say epistle and psalter, it was not queer that one night, when the election had gone awfully, and the men were as blue as that little porcelain Osiris of mine yonder, who is so blue that he cannot stand on his feet—it was not queer, I say, that they turned instinctively to "Robinson Crusoe" for relief.

Now, Robinson Crusoe was once in a very bad box indeed, and to comfort himself as well as he could, and to set the good against the evil, that he might have something to distinguish his case from worse, he stated impartially, like debtor and creditor, the comforts and miseries, thus :

Evil.	Good.
I am cast upon a horrible desolate island, void of all hope of recovery.	But I am alive, and not drowned as all my ship's company were.
I am singled out and separated, as it were, from all the world, to be miserable.	But I am singled out, too, from the ship's crew to be spared from death.

And so the debtor and creditor account goes on.

Julia Hackmatack read this aloud to them—the whole of it—and they agreed, as Robinson says, not so much for their posterity as to keep their thoughts from daily poring on their trials, that for each family they would make such a balance. What might not come of it? Perhaps a partial, nay, perhaps a perfect, cure!

So they determined that on the instant they would go to work, and thus two in the smoking-room, two in the dining-room, two in George's study, and two in the parlor, they should in the next half hour make up their lists of good and evil. Here are the results:

FREDERIC AND MARY INGHAM.

Good.	Evil.
We have three nice boys and three nice girls.	But the door-bell rings all the time.
We have enough to eat, drink, and wear.	But the coal bill is awful, and the Larrabee furnace has given out. The firm that made it has gone up, and no castings can be had to mend it.
We have more books than we can read, and do not care to read many newspapers.	But our friends borrow our books, and only return odd volumes.
We have many very dear friends—enough.	But we are behindhand 143 names on our lists of calls.
We have health in our family.	But the children may be sick. The Lowndes children are.
We seem to be of some use in the world.	But Mrs. Hogarth has left Fred $200 for the poor, and he is afraid he shall spend it wrong.
	The country has gone to the dogs.

GEORGE AND ANNA HALIBURTON.

Good.	Evil.
We have a nice home in town, and one in Sharon, and a seashore place at Little Gau, and we have friends enough to fill them.	You cannot give a cup of coffee to a beggar but he sends five hundred million tramps to the door.
We have some of the nicest children in the world.	A great many people call whose names we have forgotten.

IDEALS.

Good.	Evil.
We have enough to do, and not too much.	We have to give a party to all our acquaintance every year, which is horrid.
Business is good enough, though complaining.	We do not do anything we want to do, and we do a great deal that we do not want to do. George had added, "And there is no help in us." But Anna marked that out as wicked.
The children are all well.	People vote as if they were possessed.

GEORGE AND JULIA HACKMATACK.

Good.	Evil.
We have eight splendid children.	The plumbers' work always gives way at the wrong time, and the plumbers' bills are awful.
We have money enough, though we know what to do with more.	The furnace will not heat the house unless the wind is at the southwest. None of the chimneys draw well.
George will not have to go to Bahia next year.	We hate the Kydd School. The master drinks and the first assistant lies. But we live in that district; so the boys have to go there.
Tom got through with scarlet fever without being deaf.	Lucy said "commence" yesterday, Jane said "gent," Walter said "bully for you," and Alice said "nobby." And what is coming we do not know.
Dr. Witherspoon has accepted the presidency of Tiberias College in Alaska.	How long any man can live under this government I do not know.

FELIX AND FAUSTA CARTER.

Good.	Evil.
Governments are stronger every year. Money goes farther than it did.	But as the children grow bigger, their clothes cost more.
All the boys are good and well. So are the girls. They are splendid children.	But the children get no good at school, except measles, whooping-cough, and scarlet fever.

Good.	Evil.
Old Mr. Porter died last week, and Felix gets promotion in the office.	But the gas-meter lies; and the gas company wants to have it lie.
The lost volume of Fichte was left on the door-step last night by some one who rang the bell and ran away. It is rather wet, but when it is bound will look nicely.	But the Athenæum is always calling in its books to examine them, and making us say where Mr. Fred Curtis's books are. As if we cared.
The mistress of the Arabella School is dead.	But our drains smell awfully, though the Board of Health says they do not.
	We have to go to evening parties among our friends, or seem stuck up. We hate to go, and wish there were none. We had rather come here.
	The increasing worthlessness of the franchise.

With these papers they gathered all in the study just as the clock struck nine, and, in good old Boston fashion, Silas was bringing in some hot oysters. They ate the oysters, which were good—trust Anna for that—and then the women read the papers, while the smoking men smoked and pondered.

They all recognized the gravity of the situation. Still, as Julia said, they felt better already. It was like having the doctor come; you knew the worst, and could make ready for it.

They did not discuss the statements much. They had discussed them too much in severalty. They did agree that they should be left to Felix to report upon the next evening. He was, so to speak, to post them, to strike out from each side the quantities which could be eliminated, and leave the equations so simplified that the eight might determine what they should do about it—indeed, what they could do about it.

The visitors put on their "things"—how strange

that that word should once have meant " parliaments !"—kissed good-by so far as they were womanly, and went home. George Haliburton screwed down the gas, and he and his wife went to bed.

II. STRIKING THE BALANCE.

The next night they went to see Warren at the Museum. That probably helped them. After the play they met by appointment at the Carters'. Felix read his

Report.

1. NUMBER.—There are twenty-one reasons for congratulation, twenty-four for regret. But of the twenty-four, four are the same, namely, the accursed political prospect of the country. Counting that as one only, there are twenty-one on each side.

2. EVIL.—The twenty-one evils may be classified thus : political, 1 ; social, 12 ; physical, 5 ; terrors, 3.

All the physical evils would be relieved by living in a temperate climate, instead of this abomination, which is not a climate, to which our ancestors were sold by the cupidity of the Dutch.

The political evil would be ended by leaving the jurisdiction of the United States.

The social evils, which are a majority of all, would be reduced by residence in any place where there were not so many people.

The terrors properly belong to all the classes. In a decent climate, in a country not governed by its vices, and a community not crowded, the three terrors would be materially abated, if not put to an end.

Respectfully submitted, FELIX CARTER.

How they discussed it now ! Talk? I think so ! They all talked awhile, and no one listened. But they had to stop when Phenice brought in the Welsh rare-bit (good before bed, but a little indigestible, unless your conscience is stainless), and Felix then put in a word.

"Now I tell you, this is not nonsense. Why not do what Winslow and Standish and those fellows thought they were doing when they sailed ? Why not go to a climate like France, with milder winters and cooler summers than here ? You want some winter, you want some summer."

"I hate centipedes and scorpions," said Anna.

"There's no need of them. There's a place in Mexico, not a hundred miles from the sea, where you can have your temperature just as you like."

"Stuff!"

"No, it is not stuff at all," said poor Felix, eagerly. "I do not mean just one spot. But you live in this valley, you know. If you find it is growing hot, you move about a quarter of a mile to a another place higher up. If you find that hot, why you have another house a little higher. Don't you see? Then, when winter comes, you move down."

"Are there many people there?" asked Haliburton; "and do they make many calls?"

"There are a good many people, but they are a gentle set. They never quarrel. They are a little too high up for the revolutions, and there is something tranquillizing about the place ; they seldom die, none are sick, they need no aguardiente, do what the head of the village tells them to do—only he never has any occasion to tell them. They never make calls."

"I like that," said Ingham. "That patriarchal system is the true system of government."

"Where is this place?" said Anna, incredulously.

"I have been trying to remember all day, but I can't. It is in Mexico, I know. It is on this side of Mexico. It tells all about it in an old *Harper*—oh, a good many years ago—but I never bound mine ; there are always one or two missing every year. I asked Fausta to look for it, but she was busy. I thought," continued poor Felix, a little crestfallen, "one of you might remember."

No, nobody remembered ; and nobody felt much like going to the public library to look, on Carter's rather vague indications. In fact, it was a suggestion of Haliburton's which proved more popular.

Haliburton said he had not laid in his coal. They all said the same. "Now," said he, "the coal of this crowd for this winter will cost a thousand dollars, if you add in the kindling and the matches, and patching the furnace pots and sweeping the chimneys."

To this they agreed.

"It is now Wednesday. Let us start Saturday for Memphis, take a cheap boat to New Orleans, go thence to Vera Cruz by steamer, explore the ground, buy the houses if we like, and return by the time we can do without fires next spring. Our board will cost less than it would here, for it is there the beef comes from. And the thousand dollars will pay the fares both ways."

The women, with one voice, cried, "And the children?"

"Oh, yes," cried the eager adventurer. "I had forgotten the children. Well, they are all well, are they not?"

Yes ; all were well.

"Then we will take them with us as far as Yellow Springs, in Ohio, and leave them for the fall and winter terms at Antioch College. They will be enough better taught than they are at the Kydd School, and they will get no scarlet fever. Nobody is ever sick there. They will be better cared for than my children are when they are left to me, and they will be seven hundred miles nearer to us than if they were here. The little ones can go to the Model Schools, the middling ones to the Academy, and the oldest can go to college. How many are there, Felix?"

Felix said there were twenty-nine.

"Well," said the arithmetical George, "it is the cheapest place I ever knew. Why, their seniors get along for three hundred dollars a year, and squeeze more out of life than I do out of twenty thousand. The little ones won't cost at that rate. A hundred and fifty dollars for twenty-nine children for six months; how much is that, Polly?"

"Forty-three hundred and fifty dollars, of course," said she.

"I thought so. Well, don't you see, we shall save that in wages to these servants we are boarding here, of whom there are eleven, who cost us, say, six dollars a week; that is, sixty-six dollars for twenty weeks is thirteen hundred and twenty dollars. We won't buy any clothes, but live on the old ones, and make the children wear their big brothers' and sisters'. There's a saving of thirty-seven hundred dollars for thirty-seven of us. Why, we shall make money! I tell you what, if you'll do it, I'll pay all the bills till we come home. If you like, you shall then each pay me three-quarters of your last winter's accounts, and I'll charge any difference to profit and loss. But I shall make by the bargain."

The women doubted if they could be ready. But it proved they could. Still they did not start Saturday; they started Monday, in two palace-cars. They left the children, all delighted with the change, at Antioch on Wednesday—a little tempted to spend the winter there themselves ; but, this temptation well resisted, they sped on to Mexico.

III. FULFILMENT.

Such a tranquil three days on the Mississippi, which was on an autumn flood, and revealed himself as indeed King of Waters ! Such delightful three days in hospitable New Orleans ! Might it not be possible to tarry even here ? " No," cried the inexorable George. " We have put our hand to the plough. Who will turn back ?" Two days of abject wetchedness on the Gulf of Mexico. " Why were we born ? Why did we not die before we left solid land ?" And then the light-house at Vera Cruz.

" Lo, land ! and all was well."

What a splendid city ! Why had nobody told them of this queen on the sea-shore ? Red and white towers, cupolas, battlements ! It was all like a story-book. When they landed, to be sure it was not quite so big a place as they had fancied from all this show ; but for this they did not care. To land—that was enough. Had they landed on a sand spit they would have been in heaven. No more swaying to and fro as they lay in bed ; no more stumbling to and fro as they walked. They refused the amazed Mexicans who wanted them to ride to the hotel. To walk steadily was in itself a luxury.

And then, it was not long before the men had selected the little caravan of horses and mules which were to carry them on their expedition of discovery. Some valley of paradise, where a man could change his climate from midwinter to midsummer by a journey of a mile. Did the consul happen to have heard of any such valley?

Had he heard of them? He had heard of fifty. He had not, indeed, heard of much else. How could he help hearing of them?

Could the consul, then, recommend one or two valleys which might be for sale? Or was it, perhaps, impossible to buy a foothold in such an Eden?

For sale! There was nothing in the country, so far as the friend knew to whom the consul presented them, which was not for sale. Anywhere in Queretaro; or why should they not go to the Baxio? No; that was too flat and too far off. There were pretty places round Xalapa. Oh, plenty of plantations for sale! But they need not go so far. Anywhere on the rise of Chiquihiti.

Was the friend quite sure that there were no plumbers in the regions he named?

"Never a plumber in Mexico."

Any life-insurance men?

"Not one." The prudent friend did not add, "Risk too high."

Were the public schools graded schools or district schools?

"Not a public school in six provinces."

"Would the neighbors be offended if we did not call?"

"Cut your throats if you did."

Did the friend think there would be many tramps?

The friend seemed more doubtful here, but suggested that the occasional use of a six-shooter reduced the number, and gave a certain reputation to the premises where it was employed, which diminished much tramping afterward, and he said that the law did not object to this method.

They returned to a dinner of fish, for which Vera Cruz is celebrated. " If what this man says be true," said Ingham, " we must be very near heaven."

It was now in November. Oh, the glory of that ride, as they left Vera Cruz and, through a wilderness of color, jogged slowly on to their new paradise !

" Through Eden four glad couples took their way."

Higher and higher. This wonder and that. Not a blade of grass such as they ever saw before, not a chirping cricket such as they ever heard before, a hundred bright-winged birds, and not one that they had ever seen before. Higher and higher. Trees, skies, clouds, flowers, beasts, birds, insects, all new and all lovely.

The final purchase was of one small plantation, with a house large enough for a little army, yet without a stair. Oranges, lemons, pomegranates, mangoes, bananas, pineapples, coffee, sugar—what did not ripen in those perennial gardens? Half a mile above there were two smaller houses belonging to the same estate ; half a mile above, another was purchased easily. This was too cold to stay in in November, but in June and July and August the temperature would be sixty-six, without change.

They sent back the mules. A telegram from Vera Cruz brought from Boston, in fifteen days, the best books in the world, the best piano in the world, a few boxes of colors for the artists, a few reams of paper, and a few dozens of pencils for the men. And then began four months of blessed life. Never a gas bill nor a water leak, never a crack in the furnace, never a man to put in coal, never a request to speak for the benefit of the Fenians, never the necessity of attending at a primary meeting. The ladies found in their walks these gentle Mexican children, simple, happy, civil, and with the strange idea that the object for which life is given is that men may live. They came home with new wealth untold every day—of ipomœa, convolvulus, passion-flowers, and orchids. The gentlemen brought back every day a new species, even a new genus—a new illustration of evolution or a new mystery to be accounted for by the law of natural selection. Night was all sleep ; day was all life. Digestion waited upon appetite ; appetite waited upon exercise ; exercise waited upon study ; study waited upon conversation ; conversation waited upon love. Could it be that November was over? Can life run by so fast? Can it be that Christmas has come? Can we let life go by so fast? Is it possible that it is the end of January? We cannot let life go so fast. Really, is this St. Valentine's day? When ever did life go so fast?

And with the 1st of March the mules were ordered, and they moved to the next higher level. The men and women walked. And there, on the grade of a new climate, they began on a new botany, on new discoveries, and happy life found new forms as they began again.

So sped April and so sped May. Life had its battles—oh, yes, because it was life. But they were not the pettiest of battles. They were not the battles of prisoners shut up, to keep out the weather, in cells fifteen feet square. They fought, if they fought, with God's air in their veins and God's warm sunshine around them and God's blue sky above them. So they did what they could, as they wrote and read and drew and painted, as they walked and ran and swam and rode and drove, as they encouraged this peon boy and taught that peon girl, smoothed this old woman's pillow and listened to that old man's story, as they analyzed these wonderful flowers, as they tasted these wonderful fruits, as they climbed these wonderful mountains, or, at night, as they pointed the telescope through this cloudless and stainless sky.

With all their might they lived. And they were so many, and there were so many round them to whom their coming was a new being, that they lived in love, and every day drank in of the infinite elixir.

But June came. The mules are sent for again. Again they walked a quarter of a mile. And here in the little whitewashed cottage, with only a selection from the books below, with two guitars and a flute in place of the piano—here they made ready for three weeks of June. Only three weeks; for on the 29th was the Commencement at Antioch, and Jane and Walter and Florence were to take their degrees. There would need five days from Vera Cruz to reach them. And so this summer was to be spent in the North with them, before October should bring all the children and the parents to the land of the open sky.

Three busy weeks between the 1st and the 22d, in which all the pictures must be finished, Ingham's novel must be revised, Haliburton's articles completed, the new invention for measuring power must be gauged and tested, the dried flowers must be mounted and packed, the preserved fruits must be divided for the northern friends. Three happy weeks of life eventful, but life without crowding and, above all, without interruption. "Think of it," cried Felix, as they took their last walk among the lava crags, "the door-bell has not rung all this last winter!"

> "'This happy old king
> On his gate he did swing,
> Because there was never a door-bell to ring.'"

This was Julia's impromptu reply.

IV. HOME AGAIN.

So came one more journey. Why can we not go and come without this musty steamer, these odious smells, this food for dogs, and this surge—ah, how remorseless!—of the cruel sea?

But even this will end. Once more the Stars and Stripes! A land of furnaces and of water-pipes, a land of beggars and of caucuses, a land of gas-meters and of liars, a land of pasteboard and of cards, a land of etiquettes and of bad spelling, but still their country! A land of telegraphs, which told in an instant, as they landed on the levee, that all the twenty-nine were well, and begged them to be at the college on Tuesday evening, so as to see *Much Ado about Nothing*. For at Antioch they act a play the night before Commencement. A land of Pullman's palace cars. And lo! they secured sections 5 and 6, 7 and 8, in the "Mayflower." Just time to kiss the baby of one friend, and to give a basket of guavas to another, and then whir for Cincinnati and Xenia and Yellow Springs!

How beautiful were the live-oaks and the magnolias! How fresh the green of the cotton! How black the faces of the little negroes, and how beyond dispute the perfume of the baked peanuts at the stations where sometimes they had to stop for wood and water! Even the heavy pile of smoke above Cincinnati was golden with the hopes of a new-born day as they rushed up to the Ohio River, and as they crossed it. And then, the land of happy homes! It was Kapnist who said to me that the most favored places in the world were the larger villages in Ohio. He had gone everywhere, too. Xenia, and a perfect breakfast at the station, then the towers of Antioch, then the twenty-nine children waving their handkerchiefs as the train rushes in!

How much there was to tell, to show, to ask for, and to see! How much pleasure they gave with their cochineal, their mangoes, their bananas, their hatbands for the boys, and their fans for the girls! Yes; and how much more they took from nut-brown faces, from smiles beaming from ear to ear, from the boy so tall that he looked down upon his father, from the girl so womanly that you asked if her mother were not masquerading. "You rascal, Ozro, you do not pretend that those trousers were made for you? Why, my boy, you disgrace the family." "I hope not, papa; I had ninety-eight in the botany examination, passed with honors in Greek, and we beat the Buckeye Club to nothing in the return match yesterday." "You did, you little beggar?" the proud papa replied. "You ran all the better, I suppose, because you had nothing to trip you." And so on, and so on. The children did not live in paradise, perhaps, but this seems very like the kingdom come!

And after commencements and the president's party, up to the Yellow Springs platform came two unusual palaces, specially engaged. And one was named the "Valparaiso," and the other, as it happened, the "Bethlehem." And they took all the children, and by good luck Mrs. Tucker was going also, and three or four of the college girls, and they took them. So there were forty-two in all. And they sped and sped, without change of cars, save as Bethlehem visited Paradise and Paradise visited Bethlehem, till they came to New Salem, which is the station men buy tickets for, when they would go to the beach below Quonochontaug, where the eight and the twenty-nine were to make their summer home before the final emigration.

They do not live at Quonochontaug, but to that post-office are their letters sent. They live in a hamlet of their own, known to the neighbors as the Little Gau. Four large houses, whitewashed without and within, with deep piazzas all around, the roofs of which join the roofs of the houses themselves, and run up on all sides to one point above the centre. In each house a hall some twenty feet by fifty, and in the hall—what is not in the hall?—maybe a piano, maybe a fish-rod, maybe a rifle or a telescope, a volume of sermons or a volume of songs, a spinning-wheel, or a guitar, or a battledore. You might ask widely for what you needed, for study or for play, and you would find it, though it were a deep divan of Osiût or a chibouque from Stamboul—you would find it in one of these simple whitewashed halls.

Little Gau is so near the sea-shore that every day they go down to the beach to bathe, and the beach is so near the Gulf Stream that the swim is—well, perfection. Still, the first day the ladies would not swim. They had the trunks to open, they said, and the closets to arrange. And the four men and the fourteen boys went to that bath of baths alone. And as Felix, the cynic grumbler, ran races naked on the beach with his boy and the boy beat him, even Felix was heard to say, "How little man needs here below to be perfectly happy!"

And at the Little Gau they spent the months from the 4th of July to the 13th of October—two great days in history—getting ready for Mexico. New sewing machines were bought, and the fall of the stream from the lake was taught to run the treadles. No end of clothing was got ready for a country which needs none; no end of memoranda made for the last purchases; no end of lists of books prepared, which they could read in that land of leisure. And on the 14th of October, with a passing sigh, they bade good-by to boats and dogs and cows and horses and neighbors and beaches—almost to sun and moon, which had smiled on so much happiness, and went back to Boston to make the last bargains, to pay the last bills, and to say the last good-bys.

After one day of bill-paying and house-advertising and farewelling, they met at Ingham's to "tell their times." And Julia told of her farewell call on dear Mrs. Blake.

"The saint!" said she; "she does not see as well as she did. But it was just lovely there. There was the great bronze Japanese stork, which seemed so friendly, and the great vases, and her flowers as fresh as ever, and her books everywhere. She found something for Tom and Maud to play with, just as she used to for Ben and Horace. And we sat and talked of Mexico and Antioch and everything. I asked her if her eyes troubled her, and I was delighted because it seems they do not trouble her at all. She told all about Swampscot and her grandchildren. I asked her if the dust never troubled them on Gladstone Street, but she says it does not at all ; and she told all about her son's family in Hong-Kong. I asked her if the failure of Rupee and Lac annoyed them, and she said not at all, and I was so glad, for I had been so afraid for them ; and then she told about how much they were enjoying Macaulay. Then I asked her if the new anvil factory on the other side of the street did not trouble her, and she said not at all. And when I said, 'How can that be?' she said, 'Why, Julia dear, we do not let these things trouble us, don't you see? If I were you, I would not let such things trouble me.'"

George Haliburton laid down his knife as Julia told the story. "Do you remember Rabia at Mecca?"

Yes, they all remembered Rabia at Mecca :

> "O heart, weak follower of the weak,
>   That thou shouldst traverse land and sea ;
> In this far place that God to seek
>   Who long ago had come to thee!"

"Why should we not stay here, and not let these things trouble us?"

Why not, indeed?

AND THEY STAYED!

"They stayed, after all!" cried Mrs. Fréchette, when the professor finished the last chapter. "After all those butterflies and bananas and sugar-canes ; did you stay and freeze and thaw, Mrs. Hackmatack?"

"We certainly did," said Julia, "else I should not have been here."

"Well, if my husband will ever put me in a country which knows nothing of kindlings and coal-dust, and yarn, and knitting and darning, worst of all, in that country I shall stay."

And they went on, in groups, in quite eager discussion of the conclusion of the story.

Sitting far back, in the retirement of Number 3, Theodora said to Mr. Decker: "Would you have stayed or would you have gone back again?"

He was on the very edge of saying, "If you had stayed, I should have stayed, and if you had gone, I should have gone;" and as this was the exact truth, those advantages which belong to speaking the truth in all places would have followed the statement.

But, in fact, he just caught himself.

"I should—well, that is a question; why—you know I should—I suppose I should have done as the rest did."

"You give yourself very little credit for decision of character," said she, laughing. "You must read Mr. Foster's essay."

"Oh, essays will do me no good. Well, I confess, I told you that I am of no kind of use unless I am living with other people. With them and for them, I believe I ought to say, and they living with me and for me, I will say, too."

"You believe in the 'Together,'" said Julia, forgetting that he had not heard that story read.

"Why," said he, surprised, "do you know that is my chief's motto? It is on his seal ring, and it is on the letter paper of the works.

"Yes, I believe in the 'Together,' as I hardly believe in anything else. And it is clear that Mr. and Mrs. Hackmatack yonder and their crowd found that life depended, not on cocoanuts or sugar-canes, but on the more or less of love."

"Of love and of good temper," said the girl, never dreaming that he was looking through and through her, and hoping that she would divine how much he meant.

"Of love and of good temper, yes," he said, perhaps a little disappointed. "But good temper comes with love, with such love as I mean. If one of those people in the story, with all their joking and discussing—if one of those men knows and feels that the other—I don't mean the other—if he knows that Alice, or Polly, or whatever the name is—if she has rescued him from himself, or from just a bear's life with other bears—if she has given him home, and the glory of home by going into his cabin with him—and—being good to him, and kind to him, and explaining to him and cheering him up, why, he is a brute if he is ill-tempered to her, or if he is not willing to move the cabin from one place to another if she wants him to. Don't you see?"

But Theodora laughed. "I see that he might be very good-tempered, and I am afraid, poor man, he would have to be, if he treated his Polly or his Alice in that fashion. No, no, Mr. Decker, the good nature is needed on her side as well as on his side. She must sit in the cabin all day, while he is out with his flute on the sierra, catching the key-note of the 'mockingbirds.'"

"I do not see that—I do not see why she should not be at his side with her zithern."

And they both laughed. She began again: "Well, I will not have him on the sierra. She must be all day in the cabin, because it rains, oh, it rains in torrents, and he is sitting on the edge of Deadman's Gulch, holding a claim which Bob Watriss and Jim Blackeye want to run. She sees nobody and nothing for the twelve hours of every day, and all the time it rains, and the chimney smokes, and her meal is bad ; but she must have the supper warm and nice when he comes in. And she must not lose her temper."

Paul Decker looked at her with even new admiration. "You have been there," he said. "That is what the boys would say. And I am sure you did not lose yours." This, with some terror, lest he was going farther than he might.

But Theodora was unconscious of compliment. She sighed : "Ah me ! I wish I were sure of that. But you are right, Mr. Decker. She never did—my mother never did. Just as sunny and as sweet when the chimney smoked, and when there were six dirty Indians squatting round the fire, as she was on her wedding-day. And once, when I dared ask her how it was that she never once broke down, when I was as cross as a bear, she smiled with the smile of an angel, and she said to me, " Dora, dear—"

Then Theodora stopped, and she said : " No ; I don't think I ought to repeat what she said, even to you."

" Even !" The moment the words had gone, she saw what she had said, and if anybody could have seen her—her cheeks flushed fire.

Paul Decker noticed them as well—never doubt that —and he could have shouted with his exultation. But Life slides on without hitches or delays, whether young people do or do not make slips in their talk, and at this moment Hector's loud voice was heard.

" The president is distressed to observe the laxity and lack of discipline of the company. The hours are rapidly ebbing, and to-day will soon be to-morrow, or yesterday, I really forget which. Meanwhile I understand that the preparations are all made for the tableau, and Mr. Paul Decker and his company will favor us with the great historical painting of

"THE APACHE'S REVENGE."

Paul, good fellow, he had wholly forgotten the rigmarole of the programme, and he was wholly off his guard.

But he did not mean to have that party of people all staring at him and at Miss Bourn, in the deep recess of Number 3.

With the audacity of genius, he sprang forward, caught from the rack in the car the gilded axe which was part of its provision, and seized up Cæsar's feather duster in his left hand.

Then he pretended to flourish the axe over the head of Professor Wisner, and held him so firmly, that the tableau was complete. The assembly broke into applause.

What was better, no one dreamed how Paul had been occupied the moment before.

"And now," cried Hector, "we will ask Mr. Fréchette for his love story, and then the hall will be cleared for dancing."

"My love story, as it happens, is a Christmas story," said Mr. Fréchette. "I would tell it as my friend, Dr. Withers, told it to me; but as all the others have read, I am modest about talking." So he unfolded a newspaper, and read the story of

NOTHING TO GIVE.

A CHRISTMAS TALE.

Nora had learned some things at school. She had learned many more since she was tossed head foremost into that sea which we call life and was told to swim.

She had learned a great deal of human nature, and, among other things, of her own nature since she had been the head book keeper at Schweigel & Drum's.

But one thing she had not learned. She had not learned that when, on the first of January, you plan your expenses for the year, knowing what your income is to be and wishing not to exceed it, you must provide for "Monsieur L'Imprévu"—for " Mr. Unexpected."

A wise person, in laying out his time or disposing, in advance, of his money, leaves full half for the expenditures of this monster. We never expect his coming at any given moment; but, all the same, a person who has learned the lesson of life knows very well that he will come at some moment, and that he is a very expensive visitor.

Not having learned this, Nora had spent in this particular year very close to the margin, and so she had on the 20th of December just five dollars left, with which to buy her Christmas presents.

"It is not so much as I wish," said Nora; "but I will make it answer." She remembered the Japanese stores and Macy's cheap counters, and she was quite sure she could make her five dollars do. She would take leave of absence from the desk for the whole of Wednesday afternoon, would make the tour of the shops, would figure over the prices, and then in a couple of hours on Thursday she could make all her purchases.

All very fine, Nora, if " Mr. Unexpected" do not step in.

But he did step in. When Nora came home Tuesday night there was a letter. It was this letter:

MT. VERNON, December 20.

MY DEAR, DEAR NORA : I am so wretched and have no one to turn to but you. Such a poor creature am I, as I always was. And, as always, you are my only help. O Nora, what shall.I do ? He is off again, God knows where ! He was here—here in this house for four days, after his last time. O Nora, it was hell, at first ; and then I really pitied him. And then he was so wretched himself ; and he begged me to forgive him ; and he swore on his knees, and he took the Bible in his hands, that he would never touch liquor again. Then he dressed himself as well as he could, and went to the works, to beg them to take him on again. O Nora, why did I not go with him ? That noon he was seen at that horrible Kirke's saloon. They call it Hell-gate Lager, and they call it well. That night he was staggering along the canal bank, not knowing the men that met him, and, Nora, he has never been seen since ! What shall I do, Nora, and where shall I go ? There has not been a spark of fire on this hearth for four days, and I have begged all the milk I have given to the poor, dear babies. I get on with almost nothing. Write me, Nora, something and tell me how to do. I know you love me, and you are wise, and I was always foolish.

Always your own poor ANN.

This letter Nora answered by enclosing to Ann Vinton the five dollars she had reserved for her presents. She did not go to the Japanese shops, and the crowd at Macy's was the smaller by one, because Ann Vinton had written this letter.

So it was that when Christmas eve came round, Nora found herself sitting in her little room, looking into her stove, and saying to herself that she had nothing to spend for Christmas, for the first time she could remember since she was born.

As for making presents with her hands for her friends, well, Nora was not of that kind. After her day's work at Schweigel & Drum's she was in no condition to paint fans, or embroider portières, or to cut out and glue card-board. "All very fine," said Nora, aloud, "this about giving yourself to your friends. I should give myself away very soon, if I tried that." And then her poor little joke provoked her. No; they must do without poor Nora's presents this time, simply and squarely because "I've NOTHING TO GIVE."

There was a tap at the door, and, at Nora's summons, Martha Buchanan entered. She was a girl who shared with another girl the attic off the end of the entry. Nora's room was the square attic room, as large as the front parlor and only five stories above it. Nora took her room alone, and this single fact would have given a certain distinction to her among the seven girls whose lodgings were on that floor; but, to say truth, she had other ways of earning distinction, and her headship was recognized.

"Miss Afflitt, could you and would you lend me a dollar?"

Nora laughed; not cynically, even good-naturedly. "Take my purse, Martha. Take my all. I share it with you willingly," and she gave it to her.

Martha opened it, and laughed also. "Are you as hard up as that? Why, I can do better than that, Miss Afflitt. Shall I not lend you something?"

"No, dear child. There are only two devils known to me—one is drink and the other is debt. I have only to start fifteen minutes earlier every morning and walk to the store, and pay-day is on the 30th this year, when I shall be fly again." Fly was a cant word these girls had invented, or picked up from the short-hand girls they knew, who use it for another purpose.

Nora chattered on the faster, because she saw, too late, that, in condemning debt, she had censured Martha, who had come in to borrow.

But Martha took no offence. " Oh dear, I wish I were half as wise as you. But it says in the Book that half of them were wise and half were foolish, and I suppose that is the way always. What do you think I wanted the dollar for ?"

Nora could not guess, of course. Martha told her.

" You see, I have a dollar and a half. I wanted to treat a new girl there is in our store, who has been good to me ever since she came. She is in the cloak room, you know. Well, she is French, I believe—French or German ; and I was going to ask her to see Patti with me to-night, because she is sort of lonely evenings, and I—well, Miss Nora, you know I am always lonely." And poor, silly Martha's face fell and looked very sad.

Nora doubted what to do or to say. Then she was swept away by The Spirit. She determined herself to say nothing ; but the moment she had so determined The Spirit possessed her and they said together :

" Martha, I don't like to think of your going to the theatre so, with a girl you don't know much, and with no real escort of your own." And, if Nora had not feared to seem selfish, she would have added, " And on borrowed money." " Patti is all very nice when a nice large party of us go together ; or Patti would be very nice if she would come around and sing to us here ; but seems to me I would not go much to the theatre with—with perfect strangers."

" Will you go with me, Nora—I mean Miss Afflitt ? I do so hunger and thirst for the opera sometimes ;

and to-night it is 'Sonnambula.'" And she hummed an air.

"Some night, dear child, when we are not all in debt, we will make a party and go; but to-night—"

"To-night we will sit up here and read 'Miss Hester Chapone's Letters to Young Women' and top off with 'The Last Moral Considerations of an Expiring Saint.'"

Martha was erratic and whimsical, and, if a fit of indignation came on her, she did not fear to express herself.

"We will be virtuous," she said, with a sneer, "though we have no cakes and by no means any ale."

Then, as if one outburst had settled her, she started up, and said:

"Well, any way, I can get a gallery seat alone, if I cannot ask Miss Gounod. It would be too late to ask her now, if I had the dollar. And if I am alone I had as lief sit in the gallery. That is what I shall do." So she turned to leave the room.

Nora did not like this girl; she had had storm after storm with her, not unlike this squall; but she hated to have the girl go to the bad, if she could help it, and she had the feeling come over her that this was one of the crisis minutes. She spoke as before, not much knowing why she spoke or what she said.

"Martha, let me go, too? We need not read Hester Chapone."

"Oh, no," said the mad creature. "We can go to a vestry meeting and hear the Rev. Boanerges Howl's tenth lecture on the seventh city of the plain. Do let us go there together!"

"Dear Martha, do be patient. I had meant to stay

at home ; but it is stupid here, it is very stupid. If I have you with me, I shall not be afraid in the streets. Let us go out, if we only see the children flatten their noses against the toy-shop windows. Perhaps Santa Claus will give us a ride." And, on the impulse, she put on her Arctic boots and her waterproof.

" Will you go to Patti and sit in the gallery," said the girl, amazed, " just to keep me out of mischief? You are a saint."

" I did not say that," said Nora. " I said we would see what we would see."

It was one of those very, very rare Decembers when a heavy snowfall gives for once the joy of sleigh-bells for a day or two even to the crowded avenues and to Broadway, and the two girls had hardly walked a hundred paces when a great, open sleigh, crowded with exultant passengers, swept along. It was a sleigh which one of the street railways had put on, while their ploughing was yet imperfect. As it happened, a dozen people left it at that crossing.

" It is for us, Nora," cried the impetuous Martha, and she dragged her friend, not unwillingly, upon the vacant seat. The horses started again, and for the first time for years the two girls found themselves on a sleigh-ride—all the more delightful because it was absolutely impromptu. Nora felt, indeed, as if Santa Claus had started a few hours early for the special purpose of relieving her cares. For half an hour, if for no more, her impetuous friend was cared for. Martha succeeded in keeping from singing ; but she exulted wildly, by every word and gesture which was within any definition of decorum. And Nora hoped, and hoped rightly, that she was blowing off a little of her pent-up steam.

But the ride could not last forever. The children of the public can have a good deal for five cents. But even five cents comes to an end. Not far from the Battery their elegant carriage turned, and for five cents more each, Martha providing the princely entertainment, they were borne back as far as Nora dared to go.

But she was quite wrong when she left the sleigh, if she thought Martha had seen enough of the gay world. She was only the more eager.

"Oh, no, dear Miss Afflitt. Do not drag me home quite yet. Or, if you are cold, go without me. You said I might see the children flatten their noses. You know I have—I have a dollar and a quarter left. I am going to buy some tea things for some of those little wretches. They shall not look in at the windows for nothing. I had just as lief go alone."

Poor Nora! What was there for it now? It was really at that moment that this story begins.

Yes, I believe it was The Spirit which moved her. What I know is that whoever strives to will AND to do of his good pleasure always finds out how. The AND is the important word. If, besides willing, we do, it is sure that He is present with us.

Nora willed, AND did.

"Martha, dear, I am cold; but, if you will come into this *café* with me, till I am warm again, then we will go and see the children flatten their noses at Schwartz's. Come, Martha, really it is not very bad here." And she led the wild girl into the rather dingy *café*, which the "Look-up Legion" of the Church of the Disciples had opened in a cellar. "Come in, Martha. They have burned all their Chapone's letters to warm their coffee."

"Nora," said Martha, "you know you could make me go into the jaws of death, not to say the hotter place; but a Coffee House of Virtue is what I never did try before." All the same she went in.

"Not there, Martha. That is the smoking-room."

"Right you are," said the girl, laughing. "I am not yet advanced enough for cheroots. I told Ben so, last Sunday."

"Now, if you will treat," said Nora, "order me a piece of squash pie for my Christmas and a two-cent cup of coffee."

And Martha ordered them and doubled the order for herself. And Nora sat and sipped, and Martha sat and sipped, impatient.

Nora made it last as long as she could; but it would not last forever. All this time from the next room was a harsh clangor from a piano, sweet enough in tone, but horribly played by some dabster. At last, even this apology for music stopped, and the girls could hear eager discussion.

In a minute a motherly woman came into the coffee-room.

"I beg pardon, ladies; but is there anybody here who could and would play some accompaniments in 'The Messiah'? They are very simply set, and Mr. Incledon is here ready to sing for us, if any one would play."

"Do you believe her?" said Martha, excited.

"We can see," Nora said. "It is always well to test liars." She saw that The Spirit was taking care of her. "I play very ill, madam," said she to the woman ; "but I knew that music once ;" and she gathered up her gloves and asked Martha to bring her boots, and they went into the music-room.

Perhaps twenty people were assembled there. There had been more, but the jangling amateur had driven all the others away. In a little, Nora was at her seat ; the artist who was to sing had shown her what he needed, and then, with little aid from Nora—indeed, little was needed—he sang one, two, three of those exquisite airs, all inwrought now with the best words of Isaiah ; so that he who has heard Händel cannot read the prophecy without the rhythm of the music recurring. The clear tones of the distinguished artist, as of a voice from heaven, rang through all the low rooms. One and another straggler came in, from coffee-room and from billiard-room ; and thus so many crowded together that their guest ventured to propose this duet and that quartette—not all from Händel now, but from one and another of the oratorios, or from one and another opera, or sometimes from the old "Academy Collection" or the "Carmina Sacra." Whoever he was, he knew the average American audience and the average American singer. That night he had better luck than might have been expected. Nora's head was level, and she was not once confused. Whatever he placed before her she could play at sight. Now the whole assembly sang "Coronation ;" now, by some magic known to him, he devised that such a visitor could and should sing an *Ave Maria*. The roll of music he brought with him seemed Fortunatus's bag. The Legion's little book-case of music yielded treasures not guessed at. In some chorus he caught Martha's voice rich and even exuberant. Before she knew it, he had her singing in

a four-part glee, and a billiard-marker singing the bass, while Nora furnished a soprano to the words, then new, of
"Sharp cracks the rifle yonder."

Glee, hymn, catch, ballad—four-part, three-part, two-part, and parts of all sorts—succeeded quickly, till it was fairly midnight.

"Ladies and gentlemen all, I wish you a merry Christmas," he cried. "What a jolly evening we have had! and I told Brown I could only stop here for fifteen minutes! But, to tell the truth," said he, bowing to Nora, "I did not expect to find you here. We should never have done without you." Then, as he saw how the girl blushed and was really troubled, he said, laughing, "Nor that any of the others of the ladies and gentlemen of the company would honor us with their assistance. Now it is time we were all in bed," he added, "only I must sing, were it only for Santa Claus's sake, 'Behold how brightly breaks the morning!'" And he unrolled the music and placed it before Nora, and he sang the song, oh so magificently! And then they all bade each other a merry Christmas and good-night, and started home.

"Think of going to *Sonnambula*, after all, Nora," said Martha, as they unlocked the door. "You are a witch. I have found you out, and I will have you hanged some day. Dear Miss Afflitt, forgive me." Then she turned suddenly, and kissed Nora, and fell into a burst of crying, as they found their dark way up-stairs.

It was a year after, when Forefathers' day came round again, and Nora began planning for her presents. She had learned her lesson this time. She had fifty-two dollars and interest in the bank and ten in her purse.

"Where shall I be Christmas eve this year?" said she, as she looked into her stove, now a year more dingy; for never did the "Rising Sun" touch the sides of that stove.

"I wonder where my poor wild cat, Martha, is?"

At this, Draggle-tail, the maid-of-all-work, brought up two letters, which had come by the late delivery.

And Nora told her that for reward she must take a quarter of a dollar to buy her Christmas presents with. Thus Nora began, and Draggle-tail departed in delight.

Letter number one was a square, elegant thing, which looked like an invitation, and proved to be one.

First Nora took out two cards. Mrs. James Heilbron asked her, in copper-plate engraving, to be present at her daughter's wedding, at "The Church of Life Eternal," on Christmas eve. And there was also Mr. Nahum MacLeod's card. There was also a note from Miss Jessie Heilbron, who was, as it proved, the bride. Mr. MacLeod was to be the bridegroom.

JESSIE MACLEOD TO NORA AFFLITT.

DEAR MISS AFFLITT: You do not know me, but I want you all the more at my wedding. For Mr. MacLeod wants you to come, and he has told me why. If you do not know, we will tell you that evening. Always yours truly,

JESSIE HEILBRON.

"This is a Christmas present indeed," said Nora, and she fell wondering and guessing who Jessie Heilbron or Nahum MacLeod might be, so that she forgot the other letter till the tea-bell rang.

When it rang she sprang up to go to the glass, and the other letter fell upon the floor.

MARTHA BUCHANAN TO NORA AFFLITT.

Dear Miss Nora: The Heilbrons have asked me to Jessie's wedding, and Jessie says she has asked you. Pray, come. Call for me, and take me, for I am going. Dear, dear Miss Nora, I have so much to tell you and everything to thank you for.
  Truly yours,   "Foolish Martha."

And Martha's address, unknown to Nora until now, was added.

"Wonders upon wonders," said Nora, aloud, and she locked her room-door and went down to tea.

The evening came for the wedding. Nora ordered a carriage and called for Martha, as she had arranged. She was not delayed. In a moment the eager girl was at her side. So soon as the carriage door was shut, she seized Nora's hand and kissed her passionately. "Why have I not ever gone to see you, when I love you so much and am so grateful? I must not cry. Only I am so glad and I cannot help it. If my dress is spotted with tears and I look like a fright, you will know it is your fault, and I do not care. Oh, do you remember a year ago? Oh, dear Miss Afflitt, when I think what that night did for me; and when I think what might have been, for I was just wild when I asked you for that dollar."

So she began, and then, as their long ride went on, Nora was able to extort from her her story.

It was not a great story, after all. Only, as she said, that night was a crisis. The *café* was the place, the singing was the occasion. Mr. Incledon, the great singer, had spoken of her voice to his friend, Mr. Hartmann, the organist. The two had readily found her address, and had sent for her. Mr. Hartmann had tested her voice, and had advised very wisely about its training. Mme. Coppée, under whose care he had placed her, had done the best, really the best, because the kindest things, for her young charge. She had surrounded her with her other pupils. She had provided a fit place for the girl to live in. Martha moved to it while Nora was at home at New Year, and so it was that Nora had lost the trace of her. Mme. Coppée had, before long, relieved her from the daily drudgery of the shop. She had secured for her an engagement in the choir of the Church of the Disciples. "And, Nora, how could I sing there; how could I meet those lovely Price girls and that brave Miss Sansom; how could I see them, strong as they are and beautiful, all drawing their life from The Fountain; and how could I think that I could paddle my own canoe? It was seeing them, Nora, and seeing you that saved me from myself and brought me to my Leader."

The girl said this in triumph.

"Only, how graceless," she said, "never to come to you to tell you of my life and that I am oh, so happy! But, Nora, you forgive me. For it was really that I wanted to say it to you on Christmas Eve. And to think we should be riding down the avenue again together now, just as we were then."

So they came to the church, and, my dear, George Withers married the handsome, loyal man, and the lovely, true woman. And then, after the ceremony, Nora and Martha rode again to Mr. Heilbron's house, where was to be a wedding-reception. And there, in the dressing-room, as Nora arranged Martha's hair and pinned a rosebud at her breast, she could not but see the light of heaven in the girl's eyes. It was clear that no one would think "she brought a fright" downstairs with her.

And after the mothers and fathers, and uncles and aunts, and cousins-german and cousins-Swedish, and second cousins and third cousins removed had passed by the bride and bridegroom, Nora and Martha, last of all, without any usher, moved up and presented themselves. Jessie Heilbron that was, Jessie MacLeod that is, stepped forward to meet them.

"Dear Martha, you are so good to come. And this is your beautiful friend?"

"Thank you so much for coming, Miss Afflitt," said the bridegroom. "If you do not know why, she shall tell you. No," said he, "you may both hear. I will tell you now."

For no other guest followed the two girls. It was in the lull between the family party and the outside world.

"Do you believe in devils, Miss Afflitt? A year ago the devil had me. The worst man in New York came into the *café* where I saw you first, as he had come before. He had found me, as he had found me before. He asked me to go with him to hell, as he had asked me before. And I was at the door, going, with my hand on the handle, when, do you not remember, Incledon sang,

"' Behold and see.'

I heard just that strain. And I came within one of saying : ' Get thee behind me, Satan.' I did say : ' I think I will not go. I want to hear this man sing.' I put the devil behind me. I walked through to the music-room, and you were at the piano, and this little woman was behind you.

"Miss Afflitt, I knew Jessie long before, and I loved her—she knows how well ; but she had told me she would never speak to me again if I did not break with Carker. And I—I should have gone with Carker that night, if Incledon had not sung

"'Behold and see.'

"Miss Afflitt, what do you think I said to her the morning after Incledon sang?

"I said, 'Jessie, I have sent him to his own place. So help me God, I will never speak to him again;' and, Miss Afflitt, I have kept my word.

"And that is why we sent for you to-night and for Mr. Incledon to the wedding.

"Why, here he is! Mr. Incledon, you said you had never met Miss Afflitt again. I am so glad to present you."

And they began to be merry.

For this my son, who was well-nigh dead, was alive again. He had been lost and he was found.

Three happy lives, blessed of God and giving joy to man—these were the harvest, as the Spirit orders, of that lonely Christmas eve, when poor Nora had

NOTHING TO GIVE.

CHAPTER IX.

GENERAL WASHINGTON'S PIG.

AND Mr. Fréchette read so well, and with so much pathos as he closed, that once more the company were silenced, though not saddened, and fell into quiet Christmas talk for a moment, which even Hector did not care to disturb.

It was the extra conductor, who had taken our train to relieve the regular conductor at Council Bluffs, who broke the silence, and said : " I have a queer Christmas story here, which perhaps Mr. Fréchette may like to read also." And, when Mr. Fréchette hesitated, the professor, well pleased to see that all parties were joining in the entertainment, asked Mr. Cox if he would not read it himself. Mr. Cox said the professor would read it better, and so Dr. Wisner stood up again and read to the party the merrier story of

GENERAL WASHINGTON'S PIG.

I.

"*Was ist das? Was sagt er?*"

The sergeant replied that the boy was rebellious, and said the pig was his own. His father gave it to him on the 4th of July, the boy said, so that he should always remember Independence.

And the sergeant grinned a very savage grin, as he made this report to his major.

Poor little Oscar looked up at both the faces, not understanding a word of the German, in which the sergeant and the major both spoke ; but he understood well that the drift of the talk was against him.

"It is my pig!" he screamed, again ; "its name is George Washington, and when he comes here I am to give it to him—if I want to—and if I want to, I am to have it for my own. My father gave it to me on Independence Day."

Again the obsequious sergeant, with a grin, translated the words to the major. The major bade him ask Oscar where his father was now, and why he did not intervene to protect him.

Oscar, alas! mad with rage now, was only too willing to tell. His father was with his regiment. It was only last Monday that he had bidden Oscar good-by. And if sergeant and major did not look well for themselves, his father and General Mifflin, and all the army, would be down upon them, and they would rue the day when they had interfered with his pig or him.

All which Sergeant Zenger explained, as decisively as before, to Major Grenau.

"I will tell the general the story," said the major. "The pig will make a good Christmas dinner for him. As for the brat, shut him up in your guard-house for two or three days, and teach him to say, 'God save King George.'"

So poor Oscar was marched off to the guard-house, and the throat of poor piggy was cut before fifteen minutes were over.

II.

Great was the surprise in Mrs. Winds's house that day, when Oscar, the most punctual of boys, did not appear at dinner-time. And, though one and another theory was constructed to account for his absence, poor Mrs. Winds, in her heart, believed none of them. As soon as dinner was over, she arrayed herself and began passing from house to house in the village, to gather such accounts of the boy as she could. The presence of the English army in the town troubled her, but she lived just outside the billet-line, and had no one quartered on her. Her children had been diligently charged not to visit the camp on any pretence, and to have nothing to do with the soldiers. She despatched Primus in one direction, and Salome in another, to inquire of certain aunts and uncles, who might possibly have taken the boy out of town with them, and she sent Sarah down to the South Ferry to learn if the boy had strayed there to see his cousin. For the boats and the water always tempted him. For herself, she took the more practical, if more difficult duty, of house-to-house inquiry.

As the reader knows, she did not find Oscar outside the billet-line. As it happened, also, she did not find any one who could give her any assistance. Those who said they knew most proved, as always, to know least, and most of them broke down under her severe motherly cross-examination. She visited, literally, every house, and as she came nearer and nearer to the thickly-built street, all her fears were renewed lest the boy might have been tempted by the drum and fife, and violated her orders. He was a soldier's boy, alas! why should not he go where the other boys went, to see a parade? Poor Mrs. Winds! As she trudged on in the cold, she painted to herself all the shame of walking in through a crowd of tramps, camp followers and dirty Tories, to find any boy of hers! To think that one of them should be spending his afternoon in such company!

Worse than that, alas! poor mother! Into the first house where there was a billet, no less a house than Madam Maxwell's, she went with her inquiry, to receive the answer only too definite. In times of peace, Mrs. Winds, though she were the sturdy wife of an honest farmer, would have hesitated a little before she paid an afternoon visit to Madam Maxwell. But war breaks down pasteboard distinctions; and since war came Madam Maxwell had more than once needed Mrs. Winds's help and counsel, and thus Mrs. Winds, with a certain ease, put her questions to the stately lady. Madam Maxwell sent at once for Darius, the negro slave, who in her husband's absence at the war, was master of the establishment, and in two minutes poor Mrs. Winds had gained the clew for following her poor boy. Darius and the rest had seen a Hessian sergeant with a pig in his arms, and had seen Oscar running madly after, defying and threatening the marauders, though he could not overtake them. Phœbe even testified, truly or not, that she had tried to stop the boy; but he would not hearken, but tore away. "He would have his pig," he had said. "It was his own pig, and his father had given it to him on Independence Day."

III.

Madam Maxwell gave excellent counsel; but Mrs. Winds was in no state to receive counsel. She could hardly wait with civility for the end of the stately speech of the dignified lady. She went in pursuit. She passed quickly up the main street, meaning, indeed, to come to the rescue in person. Since the troops arrived, she had scornfully refused to enter the town. But the gossip of the neighborhood had told her where the general was quartered; and, indeed, the instinct of a soldier's wife would have led her to the inn, which men still called the "Crown and Rose," where a sort of market-place is made by the crossing of the road which comes from the ferry into that main street, on which she was hurrying on. At the Crown and Rose, the red-cross flag indicated well enough that here were headquarters. Two Hessian sentinels undertook to parley with her; but she only addressed them in very loud and peremptory English. She made no sign of stopping, but waved them away with the disdain of Queen Katherine or of Lady Macbeth. The men had been scolded a dozen times already since they were put on duty, for one and another thing which they had done, in what they thought obedience to orders. A dozen women had come in and out with adjutant's passes. Perhaps this one would not show her pass. If she did, they knew they could not read it.

So Mrs. Winds fought her way in and was able to guess her way into the very presence of the general.

IV.

"*Was ist das? Was sagt sie?*" said the general in his turn, looking with eyes somewhat bleared, through the cloud of smoke which enveloped him and his aids.

"What is it? What does she say?" The aid, who was least stupefied by beer, and who, as it happened, knew most English of the party, asked Madam Winds to speak more slowly, and, with some difficulty, extorted the details of the story. When he had done so he turned good-naturedly enough to the general and said, "She has lost her little boy, and she wants to find him."

"Her little boy, what is that to me?" hiccoughed the general; "he is not my boy." And he laughed stupidly enough. "Tell her to go about her business."

The aid turned to make this uncivil reply a little civil.

"Tell him," said Lucretia Winds stiffly, "that if he does not know where Oscar Winds is, he can find out. Tell him I shall stay here till he does find."

And she drew one of the wicker-bottomed arm-chairs out from the wall and sat down in it in front of the fire.

"*Was ist das? Was sagt sie?*" said the general again, observing the movement more than the accent of the woman.

The aid was pretty well frightened by this time; but he explained as well as he might the substance of Lucretia Winds's defiance.

Of which the issue was, as need hardly be said, that in less than five minutes a file of red coats had taken Lucretia Winds and had marched her also to the guard-house.

V.

Madam Maxwell waited at her window, somewhat uneasily, to watch for Mrs. Winds's return. Mrs. Winds did not return, as the reader knows. Madam Maxwell became more and more uneasy. When it was nearly sundown she bade Darius send round the carriage, and Darius, who happened to find life dull and was willing to try some adventure, consented. The carriage came round in less than half an hour, and Madam Maxwell, elegantly arrayed for a visit, entered it at once. She bade Philemon, the coachman, take her at once to the house of the Rev. Mr. Spencer, the minister of the church. The distance was but a trifle, and, in a few minutes more, the dominie, as all men called him, was sitting in Madam Maxwell's carriage, in conference with her. Yet a few minutes more, and he appeared again from the parsonage with his shovel-hat of state, and dressed in an elegant winter coat trimmed with fur. Philemon was bidden to drive to the Crown and Rose, and did so. The dominie bade the sentinel say that Madam Maxwell and the Rev. Mr. Spencer wished to see the officer of the day. In a few moments they were ushered into the same room from which Mrs. Winds had been so unceremoniously ejected.

The general was still there. It must be confessed that the Hessian beer was not light, and that he was more stolid even than when Mrs. Winds parted from him. Madam Maxwell had taken the dominie with her, with the double hope, first, that his dignity and the respect due his cloth would carry some weight in the interview; second, with a vague feeling that the Latin language might be the medium of communication with the general. She had heard her father say that Sir Robert Walpole talked Latin with George the First.

In fact, Mr. Spencer began his courtly address to the aid by saying, "*Salve, Domine,*" as he bowed respectfully. But the German had not the least idea what he meant, and, in fact, spoke English quite well enough for all purposes of the interview.

The dominie explained that they had come in search of Mrs. Winds. In perfect good faith, the officer expressed his ignorance and surprise. It really did not occur to him that people whose social rank he apprehended from the first moment had anything in common with the farmer's wife, whom he had early in the afternoon sent out to the lock-up. With no wish to deceive, he said that he knew nothing of the lady they sought, and intimated, as people in office are apt to do, that they had both come to the wrong bureau. The dominie turned to Madam Maxwell for instructions, somewhat relieved to find that he could conduct the conversation in honest English.

Madam Maxwell hated all Hessians. She suspected a lie. With great sternness she told the dominie what Darius had told her : that Mrs. Winds had been seen to enter the Crown and Rose two hours before. As it happened, Darius had no knowledge of her method of departure, which had been conducted with some privacy.

The adjutant was puzzled ; called an orderly and spoke in German, and asked one or two questions again. Of course, he perceived in a moment more that the other woman, resolute or crazy, who had announced her intention of waiting for her son in the general's office, was the person whom his guests were seeking. Half amused, he told the dominie, only too frankly, where the prisoner was. Of course, Madam Maxwell heard the explanation.

She rose to her full height. " Mistress Winds in your filthy guard-house !" she cried indignantly. " It is an infamy. Give an order for her release immediately."

Mr. Spencer knew very well that it was not by such language that a Hessian adjutant was to be led. He did his best to soothe his principal, and he succeeded so far as to make her sit down and listen, for a moment, to his advocacy of her cause.

The dominie felt all the importance of the crisis.

In a vague hope that the general might understand him, he turned to him and began with the best pronunciation of Princeton, to address both officers in Latin.

"*Si placet vobis, Domini,*" he said, somewhat confidently. But the amazement on the adjutant's face controlled him, and he went on in more hurried English.

"I assure you, gentlemen, I assure you, my lords," for the "*Domini*" still stuck in his head, "these are our most respectable citizens. Captain Winds and Colonel Maxwell are two of our most worthy citizens. These ladies are both worthy of your entire consideration."

The officer tapped impatiently with his foot upon the floor.

"Mrs. Maxwell wishes to explain to the general that the mother is well-nigh beside herself, because she has lost her child. Have not you a child? Has not the general a child?" said the dominie, rising to pathos.

"No brats have I; no brats have the general," cried the officer, impatiently.

"This is one free country, indeed," he said, rising from his chair. The boys expect His Majesty's officers to find their pigs! The crazy women expect His Majesty's officers to find their boys! The ladies of the court expect His Majesty's officers to find the crazy women! And I suppose next I shall have His Honor the Burgomaster, and His Excellency the Swineherd, coming here to inquire what has become of the fine lady and the court preacher."

He moved his hand toward the door, to intimate that

the interview was ended ; called an orderly, bade him put a log of wood upon the fire, and sat down, turning his back to his visitors.

The dominie saw the meaning of the adjutant, and in one rash moment sealed his own fate. He crossed the room, and, with a quick, almost impetuous, gesture, seized the hand of the general, and cried eagerly and in a loud voice, because he spoke to a man of another nation :

"*Audito, audito, obsecro, domini, verba labrorum,*" " Hear me, hear me, sir, I beg you, these words of my lips." But he went no further. The general was stupid with beer, almost to the point of incompetency, quite to that of fatuity. Either because he was drunk enough to think himself attacked, or because he was angry enough to think himself insulted, he struck with his fist a square blow in the dominie's face, and seized him by the collar of his coat.

Madam Maxwell rushed forward, she hardly knew why. The orderly flung down his log and threw himself upon both of them. The adjutant turned at the noise, rushed across the room, and in his action threw down the table on which the candles stood. The sun had already set, and the red fire gave the only light upon the scene.

The voice of the general, mingling imprecations and command, called in the officer of the day and a file of soldiers. By this time the orderly had the parson's hands tightly held behind him.

The general gave the soldiers some very peremptory and profane directions ; and, in a minute more, the parson and Madam Maxwell in their turn were marched to the guard-house to spend the night in company with Mrs. Winds and with Oscar.

VI.

So easily did it happen, or so hardly, as the reader may choose to have it, that Mrs. Winds and her son, Madam Maxwell and her minister spent their Christmas together in the school-house, where Oscar had often been whipped, and where the dominie had often heard the catechism of the children. The officer in charge was, perhaps, one of the few people on that outpost who was thoroughly sober as Christmas day came in. He had been annoyed when Oscar was brought to him, angry when Mrs. Winds came, and now was fairly horrified when Madam Maxwell and the dominie were brought in. He knew quite enough of the temper of the people to know that such an insult was enough to rouse them to bring the whole building about his head, if only every white man in the town, as he well knew, had not been away under Colonel Maxwell's command. And he was soldier enough and gentleman enough to know that such retaliation was well deserved. He did his best, therefore, to make his prisoners comfortable. When Darius arrived, soon after his mistress, the major did not repress his suggestion that he could bring down from the manse and from the mansion something for the supper and the other comforts of all parties. Darius had served with his master in other wars ; and although, to his rage, he was now regarded as quite too old to take the field again, he had not forgotten that the commissariat is the most important single element in any campaign.

Still it would be absurd to say that either of the three rescuers slept much that night. As for Oscar, not rescued after all, he slept as well as even the poor pig had ever slept, who had been the unwilling cause of the whole calamity. Oscar had had appetite quite sufficient for the supper, even sumptuous, which Darius had brought down to the guard-house. He had proposed, unsuccessfully, to his mother that they should play school with these admirable appurtenances, of a real rod and real benches, and he had even shyly intimated that the dominie could hear them both say the catechism. But his mother had no heart for such amusement, at best but sombre. To Oscar, since her arrival, the imprisonment had wholly ceased to be a punishment. Indeed, while the school-house was detestable to him at the regular hour and in the proper way, there was a wild delight to him now, that he could sleep in the master's chair if he would, or dance from bench to bench, not blamed. He slept the sleep of childhood, and waked to a boy's indifference as to the future.

And, in the morning, the "incident would have been exhausted," perhaps, as our French friends say, had it not been Christmas day. But alas! when the major himself repaired to headquarters to obtain some sort of permission to release his captives, he found no one in a condition to give it.

The preparations for Christmas made by the general and by the headquarters' staff began so early, and the drinking they had thought necessary had proved so deep, that the subordinate officers even had soon found themselves without oversight, and had followed the welcome example of their seniors. To the poor major, as he entered the Crown and Rose, it was clear enough that those who were not dead drunk were dead asleep, and that he must act on his own responsibility. Alas! he knew too well his general's temper when he waked from such sleep, and, knowing that, he dared not set his prisoners at large. It was only too far probable that the general might have, the next day, some recollection of his prisoners and ask what had become of them.

So Darius brought down to the school-house the rabbit pie which Madam Maxwell had garnished with her own hands for a Christmas breakfast piece, with tarts, cakes, waffles, and other dainties, enough for twenty people, and, by the major's permission, himself entered, for the first time, the place of confinement, and spread these viands on the schoolmaster's table. His own proposition was that the whole party should escape from the back window; and he explained, only too loudly, the means by which he and Primus would assist and cover this manœuvre. But Madam Maxwell and the dominie were still on the high ropes of indignation. "They have haled us to prison openly and uncondemned, being Romans—I mean Britons—I mean Americans," said the parson, in an oratory which failed him a little at the close, " and now do they put us out privily. Nay verily, let them come themselves and fetch us out." And it was all in vain for Darius to suggest that both the general and the officer-of-the-day were quite too drunk to do any such thing.

Darius had to satisfy himself, therefore, when noonday came, by placing his ladder at the large window of the school-house, and by this inconvenient route bringing up the roast goose, the mince pies, and the Marlboroughs, and the other delicacies which were to make the Christmas dinner of the prisoners. The major would have made no difficulty about receiving them through the door in the ground floor. But seeing that the stealthy route pleased the negro, he kept himself and his sentinels discreetly out of the way. When the dinner was served the parson so far relented as to ask the major and his aid to join them, which they were not sorry to do. All parties had better appetites than might have been feared. And when the soldiers at last withdrew the parson compelled the two ladies to join him in a modest glass of Madeira, as he drank " Long life to General Washington, and confusion to the King of England."

Neither Mrs. Winds nor Madam Maxwell would have believed that Christmas day could be made to pass by so quickly in a school-house. But the sun seemed to set earlier than ever. Darius's stately sconces from the manor-house gave but little light after all. A grim, quiet snow-storm had begun without. The ladies felt now the loss of last night's sleep. Darius had made better preparation for their comfort, and they slept soundly. Even the parson, after adjusting for the fourth time the language of his memorial to the Continental Congress, on the indignity which he had suffered, lost the connection of his thought, and slept as soundly as they.

VII.

Trrrrr....! Rat-tat-tat! Boum, boum, boum!
" Mein Gott! was ist das? 'S-Waffen, 'S-Waffen!"

The major had just time to utter these cries, his aid, who was wrapped in a blanket and asleep on the floor, had just staggered to his seat and was searching for his sabre, when, with a crash, the door of the school-house flew open, and a file of snow-white soldiers dashed in.

" Prisoners," cried the first, carrying his bayonet sharply in advance. " Surrender!"

The major threw up his hand in military salute, as token that he made no resistance, and bade his aid submit as well. As one and another Hessian private straggled in from the back room, where they had been piled together, their commander bade them lay down such arms as they had.

Maxwell, the American officer in command, asked if there were any troops up-stairs.

"*Drei Gefangene*," said the major, and Maxwell was philologist and soldier enough to guess that this meant "three prisoners." He ran up in person to relieve them, and, to his amazement, rushed into the arms of his frightened wife!

The prisoners had heard the alarm; had supposed that there was a drunken fight in the street, and were wondering if their last hour was come.

VIII.

The snow was quite too deep for Madam Maxwell or for Mrs. Winds to attempt to walk home. But with a few minutes' delay, Philemon arrived with the same equipage which had served for the unfortunate visit to the Crown and Rose.

As Colonel Maxwell, with the two ladies and the little boy, drove rapidly through the street, a detail of soldiers bearing a body on stretchers met them. Maxwell waved his hand to the sergeant in command, and stopped Philemon.

"It is he! it is he!" said each of the women, as they saw the white face which looked upward, so silent, just snatching breath, from the Hessian soldier's cloak.

This was, indeed, General Rall, who had sentenced them to their prison. He had staggered out from the Crown and Rose, and mounted his horse, only to ride far enough along the street to meet a soldier's death.

"Indeed, Maxwell, I would stay a month, as you know, gladly, at another time. But to-day!"
Thus did General Washington answer Colonel Maxwell's eager invitation that he and the staff should dine with him.

"General," said the colonel, in reply, "you must dine somewhere. These fellows will be marched off not before three. Our rear guard will not leave an hour before four. If you do not come, Darius here will cut his throat. My wife and my girls will die, and on your head be it.

Washington laughed, relented, and the staff, not unwilling, left the rather dubious hospitality of the Crown and Rose.

Philemon had the joy, not to be described, of driving his four beloved bays, whom he had rescued from Hessian captivity, as in slow movement the colonel's open sleigh bore Washington, Sullivan, Reed and the black man's master, through a throng of admiring women, children, negroes and soldiers, all cheering and rejoicing.

Madam Maxwell, in her brocade of ceremony, received the distinguished party. Good Mistress Winds, her companion in adversity, was not far away.

Nor was the repast long withheld. "In these times of war we can wait for no one," said the proud colonel.

The dominie's blessing covered wide ground. It alluded to the captivity of the Israelites, and to their redemption by Moses, to the imprisonment of Paul and Silas, and the earthquake which shook the prison.

At last he said, " Amen !"

Darius had not dared till then to take the pig from the fire. He knew the dominie too well.

Then he brought his largest platter, with the pig cooked whole, holding a large carrot between his ivory teeth.

He placed him before General Washington.

" General," said Maxwell, standing, " let me introduce to you your own pig." And he told the general the story.

" Where is the boy, where is the boy ?" cried the general, laughing.

Oscar appeared, blushing to his hair.

" My lad," said Washington, " it is not every boy who can give up his pig for his country, or defy a Hessian general at his headquarters. Will you drill all the boys in Trenton, my lad, that I may have them ready when I need them ?"

Oscar stammered out his willingness.

Five years after, as Washington, with Rochambeau, and the brilliant staff which attended both, rode away from the dusty field at Yorktown, where the " great atonement" had been made in the great surrender, the great chief beckoned to his youngest aid, Lieutenant Winds.

A handsome, beardless boy rode up and saluted.

" Oscar," said the general, " I think your pig is paid for !"

As the professor read, Hector had withdrawn Mrs. Fréchette for a minute, and they had conferred.

"Ladies and gentlemen," he cried, when the story was done, "the exercises will close with 'Old Hundred.'" And everybody sang :

"From all that dwell below the skies."

And the snow men shook hands and left the palace, and most of the rest of the party. Only Hector hinted to a few of the forward passengers that Christmas was not quite over yet. When there were only ten or fifteen of us left in the car, he clapped his hands, and said :

"I was obliged to wait till we had a little more space. We will conclude our Christmas with ' Blindman's-Buff in a Pullman.'"

On the instant he leaped upon his seat, bandaged his eyes, began to count a hundred, giving all of us warning that at the "hundred" he should break loose upon us all.

Oh, the wild rebel rout that followed ! The crazy difficulty of stepping out of his way from seat to seat, avoiding and yet seeking the passage-way, and the multiplication, indeed, tenfold of the usual perplexity, of the game by interweaving it with the perplexities of palace life. The handkerchief changed a dozen times before the game came to an end, from the mere bodily exhaustion of us who had been laughing ourselves into tears, as we wildly leaped from section to section.

"Good-night all, good-night all. Where will the morning find us ?"

CHAPTER THE LAST.

PAUL DECKER did not go to bed early. He sought out for himself a lonely nook in front of the trunks in the baggage-car, where, on a three-legged chair, he reflected, and considered the position:

"*Even* to you," she had said. "Even." This was the only word by which she had intimated that he was in any way different to her from any other man who lived.

And it was not forty-eight hours since he first saw her, since he lifted her in his arms and carried her some twenty paces to a chair.

"Even to you."

Perhaps she would leave the train at Council Bluffs. Something had been said of Council Bluffs.

Should he not leave it there also?

What should he say, if he did?

Should he say, "Miss Bourn, I do not like to have you travel alone in winter. If you please, I will take my ticket to the place you are going to, if you will only tell me where it is."

Should he say—good Heaven! why might he not say—"Miss Bourn, I will stay in that place till I die, if you stay there"?

If only he had said that when the story of "Ideals" was finished, why he would now know where he was.

And if she had been **not** displeased, **why** life would be life, and all would **be well.**

But what if she had been displeased, if she had been wounded, as of course she would be wounded—she had not known him two whole days. She would have been hurt or angry, and she would have had a right to be angry.

It was better that he had not spoken.

But if—

How would it do to ask Mr. Van Sandfoord, or, perhaps, Mrs. Fréchette? She had more experience, and, with all her fun, she was evidently genuine, good and true.

Yes; in the morning, after breakfast, Paul would ask Mrs. Fréchette.

But if only the drift would last a month!

Perhaps it would. That would be the kingdom of Heaven.

And Theodora?

Cæsar made up number three first of all. And Theodora was first of all to bid the others good-night, and to retire behind her curtains.

But not to sleep.

What a goose she had been.

"*Even* to you." Did Mr. Decker think her a flirt or a fool? They had not seen each other two days, and yet she had spoken as if he were her brother, or her cousin—nay, had spoken as if she were going to make him her confidant.

Well, there was one comfort. He would leave the train the next day, and he would never see her again nor she him.

Would he never see her again?

Was she not sure as certainty, in her heart of hearts, that he would see her somehow and somewhere?

Ah, Theodora! it is dark here, and if you want to blush, you may.

"Well, if he wants to find me, he will find me. Only to-morrow, he must not go into breakfast with us, and he must not sit with us, and I must be careful when there is reading. Yes, I can manage it. I will not be a fool to-morrow."

And then Theodora began it all over again, and dissected all these questions again, and discussed them once, twice—forty times ; but at last, poor girl, she slept. And she slept well.

And when they woke in the morning they were moving! One and another, indeed, they had had some consciousness of motion, as the morning dawned.

Yes, a party, as of giants, with ploughs and engines, not to be counted or named, had stormed up through the protected snow-sheds, had come in on the flank of the region where we had been imprisoned, and, as early as two in the morning, our men had heard their whistles, and had whistled cheerily in return. The sky was clear now, though that stiff north-wester was still packing in dry snow. None the less did two hundred men of iron throw out the snow, the plank and the rafters, which were tumbled in confusion together. Steadily and surely the giants drove the heavy ploughs through the drift. And at last Goliath, panting, faced Titan, gasping, and all men and angels knew that the TRACK WAS CLEAR !

Quick work then, as all these giants together united their forces to bear the unconscious Christmas party to Plum Creek and Gibbon, to Columbus and Omaha, and to the outward world.

BREAKFAST.

And Theodora, sandwiched close between Mary and Mrs. Fréchette, goes into the breakfast-room.
Yes, and Paul Decker makes no effort to join them. Is he perhaps offended? "*Even to you.*"
She loitered at breakfast as long as she dared.
After breakfast Mrs. Fréchette and Mary would sit together talking confidentially, so that poor Paul Decker, who hung round, could not join them. Yet he did not leave the car. Theodora stayed in the state-room on some pretence of looking in her box, till Cæsar turned her out.
Paul had to speak to her, for there was no one else at that end of the car.
He. Good-morning.
She. Good-morning.
He. I hope you slept well. That is—I was glad Mrs. Fréchette said she slept well. We are going on again.
She. Yes, we are going on again.
(Pause.)
He. You are glad we are going on again?
She. Oh, yes, I believe—yes—oh, yes, every one is glad we are going on again.
He (*very glum*). I am not glad we are going on again.
(Pause.)
He. How busy the ladies seem!
She. Yes, they seem very busy.
He. Are they old friends?
She. I do not know.
(Pause.)
He. It has done snowing.

She (*looking out of the window*). Yes, it has done snowing.

He. It snowed very hard.

She. Yes.

(Pause.)

He. Have you friends at Council Bluffs or Omaha?

She (*starting*). Oh, no, I do not know any one at Council Bluffs or at Omaha, either.

Cæsar (*loudly*). What lady or gentleman has dropped a baggage check? Here's a check some gentleman has lost or some lady.

Mrs. Fréchette. It was I. I always lose them. Let me see it, Cæsar. (*Looks at the check.*) No, it's for PIQUA, PIQUA, OHIO.

Paul Decker. Then it is mine; how careless I am!

Theodora Bourn. No, it is mine. I put it in my pocket, and it is not there—for my large trunk. I gave my other check to you, Mr. Van Sandfoord, and the box is here.

Paul. Piqua? You? I am going to Piqua.

Theodora. Are you going to Piqua? Who do you know at Piqua?

Paul. I? Piqua is my home. My father is Decker, of Decker & Strange.

Theodora. And Strange is my uncle's name—it is where I shall spend the winter.

THE END.

www.ingramcontent.com/pod-product-compliance
Lightning Source LLC
Chambersburg PA
CBHW032008230426
43672CB00010B/2291